The Longest War

The Longest War

NORTHERN IRELAND'S TROUBLED HISTORY

Marc Mulholland

OXFORD
UNIVERSITY PRESS

OXFORD
UNIVERSITY PRESS

Great Clarendon Street, Oxford OX2 6DP

Oxford University Press is a department of the University of Oxford.
It furthers the University's objective of excellence in research, scholarship,
and education by publishing worldwide in

Oxford New York

Auckland Bangkok Buenos Aires Cape Town Chennai
Dar es Salaam Delhi Hong Kong Istanbul Karachi Kolkata
Kuala Lumpur Madrid Melbourne Mexico City Mumbai Nairobi
São Paulo Shanghai Singapore Taipei Tokyo Toronto

and an associated company in Berlin

Oxford is a registered trade mark of Oxford University Press
in the UK and in certain other countries

Published in the United States
by Oxford University Press Inc., New York

British Library Cataloguing in Publication Data
Data available

Library of Congress Cataloging in Publication Data
Data available
ISBN 0–19–280292–5

1 3 5 7 9 10 8 6 4 2

Typeset by RefineCatch Ltd, Bungay, Suffolk
Printed in Spain by
Book Print S.L., Barcelona

Preface and Acknowledgements

The Troubles that broke out in Northern Ireland in 1968 proved that even liberal democratic institutions and a standard of living enviable in all but the wealthiest countries were no proof against ethnic conflict in the contemporary age. In a multicultural world, the Troubles raised profound questions regarding the willingness of peoples to live with one another. The ability of law-bound states to cope with severe public disorder under the glare of international attention was sorely tested.

This introduction takes a historical perspective, but in doing so it does not suggest that the conflict is primeval or beyond reason. That Catholics in Ulster feel Irish, and Protestants feel British, and that both countenance violence to vindicate their identities, is not peculiar. The twentieth century attests to the willingness of many peoples to fight, kill, and die to preserve their national way of life. This nationalism does not have a very long history. In the pre-modern age 'nation' meant little more, often less, than religion, clan, or region. But nor is it yet a thing of the past. Almost every state in the world bases itself upon a shared sense of belonging and mutual obligation that is patriotic or nationalistic. It is hard to imagine democracy operating otherwise. Almost every government strives to defend its national culture against erosion, and puts the welfare of its people before all.

Northern Ireland's tragedy is that its people have not been

able to agree upon a common identity. Rather than stand by each other, they compete. Being so alike—in language, appearance, and broad culture—they cling tenaciously to that which marks them out. The successful consolidation of either British unionism or Irish nationalism, it is feared, will submerge the other. Other people's identity is secure because it is buttressed by a state. Their shared nationalism is often mere background to the more important pursuit of personal development. In Northern Ireland, that luxury has been lacking. Neither nationalists nor unionists feel they may rest easy. Everyone who feels part of a community, and would defend the privilege of that belonging, can identify with Ulster's plight.

My thanks to Senia Paseta, Roy Foster, Richard Michaelis, and Rachel Buxton for discussing with me some ideas here presented. I wish to thank also the staff of OUP for their careful attention. Victoria Lill has stoically listened to my moiderings on Northern Ireland, for which I am grateful. This book is dedicated to Ita and Dominic, my parents.

Marc Mulholland, 2001

Contents

List of Illustrations — ix

1 Divided Ulster: From Plantation to Partition — 1

2 Home Rule in Ulster: Stormont's Record — 38

3 Life Cheapens: The Descent into War — 67

4 The Long War — 114

5 The Long 'Peace' — 155

6 Conclusion — 189

References — 191

Further Reading — 195

Index — 197

List of Illustrations

1. Massacre of Protestants at Portadown, 1641   5
   Fotomas Index

2. 1886 riots in Belfast   16
   Illustrated London News, National Library of Ireland

3. Bonar Law inspects the Ulster Volunteer Force   22
   House of Lords Records Office

4. Stormont Building, with Carson statue in foreground   39
   Northern Ireland Tourist Board

5. County map of Northern Ireland   56
   Northern Ireland Since 1945 (Longman Group UK, 1991)

6. Troops arrive in Belfast, 1969   75
   Syndication International

7. IRA man, Joe McCann, silhouetted, at the Markets, Belfast   96
   Pacemaker Press International, Belfast

8. Provo 'Loose talk costs lives' poster   100

9. Ulster Defence Association parade outside Belfast City
   Hall, 27 May 1972   109
   Syndication International

10. Civilian searched by army, David Barzilay   123
    The British Army in Ulster, vol 3, Century Books, 1978, p. 48

11. Waterfront Hall, Lanyon Place   126
    Dnausers.d-n-a.net/dnetGOjg/NI/Belfast.htm

12. Bobby Sands   133
    Pacemaker Press International, Belfast

13. King Billy mural   136
    http:/cain.ulst.ac.uk/bibdbs/murals/lmural1.htm#kb.—with
    'Murals' box

14. IRA mural   137
    http:/cain.ulst.ac.uk/bibdbs/murals/plate37.htm#37—with
    'Murals' box

15. Thatcher and FitzGerald shake hands on signing of
    Anglo-Irish Agreement, November 1986   147
    Northern Ireland Government Information Service

16. Sinn Féin 'Fight Censorship' poster   166

17. Religious spread map of Belfast   169
    Northern Ireland Since 1945 (Longman Group UK, 1991)

18. Cover of the Good Friday Agreement   174

19. Northern Ireland Executive, at 'cabinet table', *c.*2000   179
    Pacemaker Press International, Belfast

Divided Ulster: From Plantation to Partition

Why have divisions dating from the Reformation of the sixteenth century and the plantations and religious wars of the seventeenth century persisted through Enlightenment, revolution, famine, Industrial Revolution, and mass democratic politics?

Ulster is remarkable for the tenacity of its communal divide. Sectarian patterns of conflict have reproduced through time and adapted to changed circumstances. Post-plantation there has been negligible migration into Ulster, and communities have maintained a remarkable level of integrity. Intermarriage is very rare. Only about 5 per cent of marriages cross the communal divide, and in these cases husbands usually sever connections with their own community. Patterns of landholding (poor highlands in Catholic hands, fertile lowlands in Protestant), even down to the level of family farms, have been stable over generations. The hinterlands of Coleraine, North Down, and North Antrim are overwhelmingly Protestant. Mountainous ground, the northern glens of Antrim, the Sperrins, the Mournes, the fews and ex-marshlands around Lough Neagh (Aghagallon, Coalisland, Toomebridge), are largely Catholic. With Ireland,

and thus Ulster, sheltered from the storms of total war and ethnic centrifuge characteristic of Europe in the Age of Catastrophe (1914–45), discrete communities were able to exist cheek by jowl, competitively asserting their incompatible versions of imagined community, yet never forcing a resolution.

Plantation

Ulster, comprising the nine counties of Antrim, Down, Tyrone, Armagh, Fermanagh, and Londonderry (present-day Northern Ireland), Cavan, Monaghan, and Donegal (now part of the Republic of Ireland), was until the plantation of Ulster culturally if not politically at one with Gaelic Ireland. Its natural defensive features made English subjugation of this region difficult, though, as Scotland was only nine miles distant at the narrowest stretch of channel, lowland settlers did filter in. The 1542 declaration of Henry VIII 'That the King of England, His Heirs, and Successors be Kings of Ireland ... for ever ... united and knit to the imperial crown and realm of England' indicated Tudor determination that the island be united forcefully under the crown. Only at Elizabeth's death, in 1603, was Ulster finally brought to heel.

English warfare employed a razed-earth policy to 'break the hearts' of those who resisted, and the result was a collapse of local population through famine. This allowed for a bold experiment in pacification—plantation. In 1606 Scottish settlers were 'planted' in the Ards peninsula area of Ulster. From 1608, following the flight to Europe of the Ulster Gaelic aristocratic elite, English and Scottish 'undertakers' were granted the land on the condition that they acted as a garrison. They were to guard against native resistance and build a society based upon protestantism, English law, and (in contrast to Gaelic pastoralism) settled agriculture. The plantation was a considerable success, the settlers proving industrious and determined. The Catholic peasantry abandoned by their Gaelic lords accepted with varying degrees of sullenness the presence of the newcomers. They may have simply swapped masters, but there was much hostility to the hegemony of upstart Protestants, with all the dilution of social prestige that involved in an intensely status-conscious society.

Wars of religion

As is often the case, English politics unsettled Irish circumstances. The failure of King Charles I in war opened the way to his being challenged by a puritanical, i.e. strictly Protestant, parliament. Fearing the consequences of Puritan rule, Catholic Ireland in 1641 rose in revolt, pledging allegiance to the embattled monarchy. Thus a pattern of Irish Catholic allegiance to the English monarchy—shot through, admittedly, with a strident catholicism and definite Hibernian patriotism—was established. This, rather than modern nationalism, continued to be the dominant tendency amongst Irish and Ulster Catholics into the eighteenth century.

The 1641 rebellion briefly veered into an onslaught
against the settlers in Ulster. Reports of massacre, rather
exaggerated, outraged Protestants throughout the British
Isles. Dramatic eyewitness accounts spoke of Catholic atrocities. Mr Hierome, a 'Minister of God's Word', recounted how
the rebels attacked 'a Town inhabited of English, and slew
them in a cruel manner, without mercy, to the number of
above 20 families, men, women and children. One woman,
above the rest, they hanged at her own door with her children, by the hair of the head, and afterwards burned up the
whole town with fire.' Such horrible tales motivated a harsh
vengeance by Cromwell in the late 1640s. When he stormed
Drogheda (north of Dublin) in 1649, Cromwell had the
entire garrison slaughtered and exulted over 'a righteous
judgment of God upon these barbarous wretches'. The
depredations of Cromwell's soldiers left a bitter and lasting
legacy.

The English Civil War failed conclusively to resolve
tension between a religiously moderate monarchy in-
clining towards the political absolutism of Catholic Europe,
and a gentry pulled towards stricter protestantism and
restraints on monarchical power. In 1689, year of the
Glorious Revolution, the Catholic James II was chased
from the throne by the Dutch William of Orange, with
the support of England's gentry. As James retreated to
Catholic Ireland to rally his forces, Ulster again became a
battlefield.

Londonderry city sheltered much of Ulster's Protestant
population and withstood a siege from James's forces in

1 Massacre of Protestants at Portadown, 1641. Mass-produced dramatic images such as these inflamed passions as news broadcasters were to do in the modern Troubles

1689. Reverend George Walker was in the city from the beginning of the siege on 17 April. He recorded in his diary the desperate straits of its inhabitants:

27 July: Horse flesh sold for 1/6d per pound. A quarter of dog, 5/6d, fattened by eating the bodies of the slain Irish. A dog's head, 2/6d. A cat, 4/6d. A rat, 1/-. A mouse, 6d. . . . A certain fat gentleman conceived himself in the greatest danger, and fancying that several of the garrison looked at him with a greedy eye, thought fit to hide himself for three days. . . .

30 July: [A relief ship, the *Mountjoy*, breaks the siege] to the unexpressable joy and transport of our distressed garrison, for we reckoned on two days life, and had only nine lean horses left, and among us all one pint of meal to each man.

James was ultimately defeated, but Ireland's Protestants had little reason to think that their situation might not once again become precarious. Their parliament passed a series of 'penal laws' designed to extirpate the power of catholicism in Ireland for good. The preamble to *An Act to Prevent the Further Growth of Popery* (1703) indicated their basically defensive attitude:

divers emissaries of the Church of Rome, popish priests and other persons of that persuasion, taking advantage of the weakness and ignorance of some of her Majesty's subjects, or the extreme sickness and decay of their reason, do daily endeavour to persuade and pervert them from the Protestant religion, to the great dishonour of Almighty God, the weakening of the true religion . . . to the disquieting of the peace and settlement . . . many persons so professing the popish religion have it in their power to raise divisions among Protestants, by voting in elections for members of Parliament, and also have it in their power to use other ways and means tending to the destruction of the Protestant interest in this Kingdom . . .

Penal legislation inhibited the activities of the Catholic Church and stripped wealthy Catholics of many political and social rights. In fact the long and fraught alliance between the Stuart monarchy and Irish catholicism was drawing to a close. Irish Catholics failed to rally to the Jacobite cause in

1745, when the Stuarts last made a serious attempt at comeback.

Civil war in the 1790s

The slow death of the Irish Catholic/Stuart combination against Protestant liberties created conditions for the emergence of new political alliances. As Europe basked in the Enlightenment, 'Popish superstition' and its stablemate monarchical absolutism appeared to be receding into the past. The French Revolution from 1789 looked to many Protestant liberals to be the inauguration of an era in which reason would prevail against prejudice. Wolfe Tone, a Dublin Anglican, wrote in his *Argument on Behalf of the Catholics of Ireland* (1791):

> It is not six months since the Pope was publicly burned in effigy at Paris, the capital of that Monarch who is styled the eldest son of the Church. . . . Persecution will keep alive the foolish bigotry and superstition of any sect, as the experience of five thousand years has demonstrated. Persecution bound the Irish Catholic to his priest and the Priest to the Pope; the bond of union is drawn tighter by oppression; relaxation will undo it.

Such optimism underpinned the United Irishmen organization, established in the same year to seek reform but rapidly evolving to a nationalist republican perspective. Its Protestant members believed that the new era of reason would permit Ireland to sever its connection with Britain, which was now leading the forces of counter-revolution in Europe, without risking the triumph of Catholic despotism. Its appeal was particularly marked in Ulster, where descendants of Scottish Presbyterian settlers rankled at the petty restrictions imposed upon them by the Anglican scendancy.

In the crisis-ridden conditions of the 1790s such optimism was tested to destruction. In the southern Ulster county of Armagh, Catholic and Protestant (mainly Anglican) tenant farmers were in fierce competition for land. Here the Peep O Day Boys, a Protestant peasant movement, enforced by vigilante terror penal legislation that decreed the disarming of Catholics. The difference was that Belfast had only a few hundred Catholics out of a population of thousands, whilst Armagh was evenly balanced between Catholics and Anglicans. In Belfast, one could imagine that the Catholic threat was a thing of the past; in Armagh it remained real, present, and pressing.

In 1795 the militant Loyal Orange Institution (Orange Order), its name commemorating King William of Glorious Revolution fame, superseded the Peep O Day Boys. Even more overtly political, it gained gentry and even some government backing in its terrorist campaign against 'disloyalists', both Catholic and Presbyterian. As King George III observed, 'If you want to baste an Irishman, you can easily get an Irishman to turn the spit.' The Catholic peasantry responded with their Defenders, whose ideology combined traditional Catholic themes with revolutionary rhetoric.

As sectarian conflict spiralled, the United Irishmen

suffered harsh government repression. General Lake in 1797, in the 'dragooning of Ulster', disarmed them. His targets were principally Protestant dissenters, his tool in Belfast the Militia, Catholic and Gaelic-speaking. In 1798 the United Irishmen finally rose. Here the leadership and most of the rank and file were Protestant. Henry Joy McCracken's United Army of Ulster took Larne and Antrim but was defeated. Henry Munro's Hearts of Down were crushed at Ballynahinch. Ulster Presbyterian participation was high, but the rebellions in Munster and Connacht were larger, more violent, and more definitely tinged with catholicism. One Ulster rebel leader, prior to execution, articulated the growing disillusionment of Protestant republicans: 'the Presbyterians of the North perceived too late that, if they succeeded in subverting the Constitution, they would ultimately have to contend with the Roman Catholics.'

Ulster modernizes—and stays the same

In the early nineteenth century the authority of the Catholic Church recovered dramatically and the Catholic masses acquired leaders of their own faith, notably Daniel O'Connell. In 1801 the Irish parliament was abolished and Ireland's representatives instead made up a small proportion of the United Kingdom parliament. The French Revolution had collapsed into tyranny and military defeat; Britain was again the acknowledged liberal power in the world. It enjoyed unprecedented economic success as the Industrial

Revolution gathered pace. In Ulster, the last major restrictions on Presbyterians having being lifted and sharing in the boons of industrialization, Protestants settled comfortably in support of the Union. From 1829, when Catholic MPs were permitted to attend parliament, it was apparent that only Ireland's submergence in a union with Protestant Great Britain could ensure the preservation of Ireland's Protestants from Catholic rule. Though a talisman for future nationalists, the tenuous alliance between Catholics and Protestants in the United Irishmen was at an end.

Rural confrontations between Orangemen and Catholic Ribbonmen became familiar in the nineteenth century. They clashed in 1813, at the Battle of Garvagh (in County Londonderry). More serious violence occurred in 1829, as the country pivoted towards civil war over O'Connell's campaign for Catholic emancipation. At least twenty died in clashes in counties Armagh and Tyrone. The Great Famine of 1845–50 was as bad in parts of Ulster—the south and west—as elsewhere in Ireland. Some 21 per cent of the one million famine dead came from Ulster. The opportunities for wage earning cushioned north-east Ulster, however, and sectarian animosity survived the catastrophe. In 1849 an Ulster Orange procession from Rathfriland to Castlewellan was attacked at Dolly's Brae by about a thousand Ribbonmen. The Orangemen, well armed as was usually the case in Protestant Ulster, responded and some thirty Catholics were killed.

Such disorder slowly induced the state to stop treating the Orange Order as a disorderly ally. It was becoming a threat to

Culture

The playwright Brian Friel has written, 'The Troubles are a pigmentation in our lives here, a constant irritation that detracts from real life. But life has to do with something else as well, and it's the other things which are the more permanent and real.'

Politics has undoubtedly been a preoccupation for the people of Northern Ireland, but not one easily demarcated from 'real life'. Whereas, in uncontested communities, personal identity can be taken for granted, there is no secure sense of belonging in Ulster. To display allegiance risks affronting one's neighbour. The aspirations of both communities challenge, even delegitimize, each other.

As anthropologist Rosemary Harris wrote of a pre-Troubles rural community, 'All social relationships are pervaded by a consciousness of the religious dichotomy'.

The reaction of the artist has often been one of disgust, and a desire for escape, sometimes literally through emigration. One such, the poet Louis MacNeice, wrote of his homeland:

> I hate your grandiose airs,
> Your sob stuff, your laugh and your swagger,
> Your assumption that everyone cares,
> Who is king of your castle.

Others have acknowledged that the Ulster experience is indelibly imprinted in the artist's psyche. One minor agony of growing up in Northern Ireland is the atavistic tugging of ethnic loyalty. Northern Ireland's Nobel Prize-winning poet, Seamus Heaney, though trenchantly critical of political violence, admits the element of posturing in the self-imposed duty to 'connive in civilised outrage'. The artist, with everyone else, must struggle to be fair against his own instincts:

> This principle of bearing, bearing up
> And bearing out, just having to
> Balance the intolerable in others
> Against our own . . .

Michael Longley argues that if the divisions cannot be transcended, they may interact creatively:

> The literature produced by Ulster people suggests that its inhabitants might accept this province-in-two-contexts as a cultural corridor. Unionists want to block the corridor at one end, republicans at the other. Culture, like common sense, insists it can't be done. Ulster Irishness and Ulster Britishness are bound to each other and to Ireland and to Britain. Only by promoting circulation within and through Ulster will the place ever be part of a healthy system.

This has been encouraged, with uncertain effect, by Education for Mutual Understanding (EMU), a curriculum-based programme for schools.

public order and the legitimacy of British domination. The Protestant magistracy of Ulster, notoriously partial, was reined in. In 1825 the Orange Order was banned and a succession of party procession acts between 1832 and 1844 attempted to end provocative orange coat-trailing. Following Dolly's Brae the acts were again enforced. With the rise of revolutionary nationalist Fenian agitation for an independent Irish republic, Orange pressure to stamp the territory of Ulster as loyal resumed. In 1867 William Johnson of Ballykilbeg led an illegal 'Twelfth of July' (commemorating William's victory over James) Orange demonstration at Bangor, County Down. Johnson was imprisoned for non-payment of a fine, but in November 1868 defeated two conservative candidates to top the poll for a Belfast seat in the general election. At Westminster he helped secure the repeal of the Party Processions Act in 1872 and for almost a century Orangemen marched unimpeded every 12 July. A century later, in 1985, a Unionist MP, Harold McCusker, explained the significance of this victory wrested from the state and largely against the instincts of the Orange Order's gentry leadership:

> When the men of North Armagh try to walk in Portadown it will be over a route they and their forefathers have traversed since 1796. They are not motivated out of a desire to break the law, but a sense of historic necessity to express, as they have always done, their legitimate pride in possession of their lands and liberties. They know instinctively that they only survive by their solidarity and determination.

Belfast

Just as significantly, this pattern of marching and conflict was imported into the rapidly expanding city of Belfast. The first recorded sectarian riot there was in 1813, in which two died.

Between 1835 and 1935 there were eight periods of serious rioting in Belfast—in 1835, 1857, 1864, 1872, 1886, 1898, 1920–2, and 1935. There were also two serious riots in Londonderry, in 1869 and 1884. These normally coincided with political crises, as in 1886 when riots over impending home rule led to 32 deaths and 377 injuries in Belfast alone, 86 deaths across the province.

The importation of rural violence into Belfast was based on the extraordinary growth of that city. This itself was intimately tied in with sectarian politics. In 1689 the British parliament had granted Ireland monopoly rights on the manufacture of linen, provided that all wool production, until then prospering in Ireland, take place solely in England. This was decided with the conscious intention of supporting loyalist interests. The preamble to an act passed by parliament in 1704 explicitly stated that 'the Protestant interest in Ireland ought to be supported by giving the utmost encouragement to Linen manufactures of that kingdom'.

For a period (1770s–1820) linen production spread cottage industry throughout Ireland, but there were definite advantages in Ulster. Dense population, certain environmental conditions, relatively favourable land tenure (the 'Ulster Custom'), and infusions of experience, talent, and élan from Protestant immigrants helped develop the 'Linen Triangle' of Belfast, Newry, and Dungannon. At the end of the eighteenth century a short-lived cotton industry centred around Belfast provided a model for the reorganization of the linen industry using machines. Thus Ulster proto-industry made the difficult transition to full factory manufacturing.

Cottage industries in the rest of Ireland wilted in the face of British competition.

Mechanized linen manufacturing created demand for local engineering skills and, by the 1850s, when it became cheaper to build ships from iron rather than wood, Belfast was in an ideal position to benefit from this change. It had available land, a deep-water harbour, and a vigorous harbour commission. Again from this new industry other supplementary industries, such as rope works, sprung up. In all of this the access these industries had to British markets was of key importance. Shipbuilding, which by 1915 employed one quarter of the male labour force in Ulster, depended on exports for its survival. Ulster was bound ever closer to the free-trade British empire. Belfast's population increased from 22,000 in 1806 to nearly 340,000 ninety years later. Much of this was fed by a flood of migrants, both Catholic and Protestant, from rural Ulster.

For the first time, Belfast's almost completely Protestant character was challenged. The conditions of finely balanced Armagh were, in effect, being imported into the city. In 1812 there were some 4,000 Belfast Catholics, rising to about 100,000 at the end of the century. Belfast's Catholics belonged to the lower income group. The men were generally employed as unskilled hands in foundries, chemical works, and in the shipyards and as navvies and general labourers. Women and children worked in the textile mills. By 1911, though Catholics made up about 30 per cent of the population of Belfast, only 5 per cent of all skilled workers in Belfast areas were Catholic.

2 1886 riots in Belfast. Sectarian riots in the modern Troubles often erupted at the same geographical points of friction as they had in the nineteenth century

Rural patterns of sectarian conflict were being urbanized. Nineteenth-century Belfast saw sectarianism and political intransigence become salient features of municipal life. Religious riots were the most visible sign of sectarianism, the basic causes being the Orange Order's growth (partly in response to heavy Catholic immigration), the inflammatory preaching of certain Protestant divines, denominational education, and Protestant alarm over manifestations of Irish nationalism. One evangelical preacher, Thomas Drew, reporting to a government commission on riots in 1857, indicated something of the cruel reckoning of community conflict:

> Famine, pestilence and emigration have diminished the Romish population by several millions. Thousands have left the errors of Rome for the truth of God's word; and the greater number of those who remain are of a class so priest-ridden, impulsive, uncertain, and disloyal, as to make it wonderful that statesmen should prescribe for Ireland as if it were a Popish, and not, as its real strength, worth, industry and loyalty constitute it, a great Protestant country.

Home rule

Yet some 80 per cent of Ireland's population were Catholic. Even the nine counties of Ulster had only a slim Protestant majority. The British could not indefinitely accept a definition of Ireland as essentially Protestant. William Ewart Gladstone became Liberal prime minister in 1868 affirming his 'mission . . . to pacify Ireland'. Among his first measures was the disestablishment of the Church of Ireland, a recognition that it was inappropriate to have a formal link between the state and a denomination supported only by a minority of the Irish people. This was a terrible shock to Ireland's Protestant elite, and for a brief period they doubted whether the Union as it stood really guaranteed their security.

In 1870 Isaac Butt, a Protestant lawyer who had represented Fenian prisoners and campaigned for an amnesty, founded the Home Government Association. He was no separatist; indeed his ambition was to strengthen the Union by reconciling it to Irish national aspirations. He envisaged a Dublin parliament responsible for domestic affairs, with Irish MPs continuing to sit at Westminster. The association attracted some Protestant support, mostly from the leafy suburbs of Dublin, where illusions existed that the political domination of gentlemen in a future Irish parliament would translate into an amended hegemony for the wealthy Protestants. Ulster Protestants remained sceptical. The association was replaced in 1873 by an election-orientated Home Rule League. Requiring support from a largely Catholic electorate, Butt highlighted his support for land reform and a state-funded Catholic university. The remnants of Protestant sympathy for a domestic Irish parliament faded.

After the following year's general election (the first with a secret ballot), 59 MPs were committed to home rule. Butt died in 1879, and after a further general election in 1880, the Irish Parliamentary Party (now 61 in number) elected Charles Stewart Parnell as its leader. Parnell too was a Protestant, and rather English in manner—Catholic Ireland still had something of an inferiority complex when it came to selecting its leaders—but his radicalism alienated almost all Protestants.

Parnell had made his name by leading obstructionist tactics, exploiting parliament's rules of procedure to delay business and force the government to attend to Irish grievances. Parnell's militancy found favour amongst hard-line nationalists hitherto dismissive of parliament, notably Michael Davitt, founder of the Land League, and John Devoy, a force in Irish-American Fenianism. These three formed a loose alliance known as the New Departure. Parnell became president of the Land League and, as rent strikes and 'outrages' spread over Ireland from 1879 to 1881 in a 'land war' between tenants and landlords, he stretched constitutional politics to the limit. Land agitation always found an echo in Ulster, but the barely concealed nationalist agenda of the Land League ensured its demise amongst Protestant tenant farmers there.

Gladstone's Land Act of 1881, though only a partial settlement, allowed Parnell to reorientate decisively towards clearly political objectives. A new organization, the Irish National League, switched the emphasis to home rule. Ulster's Catholics rallied to the banner but, faced with a coherent threat, Ulster Protestants—landlord, tenant; worker, capitalist; Liberal, Tory; Presbyterian and Anglican— sank their differences to defend the Union. The landed magnates of Irish landlordism found themselves at the head of Ulster's Protestant democracy. Ulster polarized. Though in the nine counties of Ulster, home rule nationalists returned a bare majority of MPs, the Prostestant north-east was solidly Unionist.

After the 1885 election the 86 members of Parnell's party held the balance of power at Westminster. Gladstone now felt that Ireland had spoken. He recognized substantial popular support for the status quo in Ulster, but was not convinced that this would be an enduring reality. As Protestants had come to accept disestablishment, he reasoned, so would they accept home rule. Gladstone introduced his first home rule bill in 1886; fierce anti-home rule riots took place in Belfast. Ninety-three of his own Liberal MPs voted against the bill, and it was defeated.

In 1889 Parnell was cited as co-respondent in a divorce case, and the scandal cost him the leadership of his party. Two years later he was dead. Gladstone's conversion to Irish home rule as the final settlement of the Irish question was no passing fad, however. In 1893 he introduced a second bill, only to see it defeated in the House of Lords. The Tories had committed themselves to the unionist cause and the Liberal party was now morally committed to home rule. Both nationalist and unionist settled down to a waiting game.

The Ulster crisis

In 1910 Britain was locked in a constitutional crisis, as a Liberal-controlled House of Commons confronted the Tory-dominated House of Lords over the legitimacy of property defying democracy. The net result of two general elections that year was a Liberal government dependent upon nationalist Irish MPs, led by John Redmond. The same year Edward Carson, a noted Dublin lawyer, became leader of the Ulster Unionist Council (UUC). The resolution of the British crisis in 1911, when the veto power of the House of Lords was removed, inaugurated an Irish crisis. The Liberals now owed it to their Irish allies to pass a home rule bill for Ireland.

The UUC had been set up in 1905 to represent all shades of unionism in the north. This represented a historic break for the movement. Until then, it had loyally placed itself behind Ireland's landlord elite—the men, after all, who had most pull at Westminster. As British politics democratized, however, so too did Ulster Unionism. The aim remained to resist home rule for Ireland in its entirety, but the trump card was the numerical weight of Ulster Protestants, even if the interests of religion, 'civility', and wealth remained important propaganda points.

The Liberal–Irish nationalist strategy was to force an unequivocal all-Ireland home rule act on Ulster Unionism. Carson's talk of armed resistance they dismissed as bluff. Once Ulster's intransigence had been faced down, concessions in the form of guarantees for religious and civil liberty, perhaps even reserved powers for Ulster representatives, could be discussed. The idea was that Irish unionism had to be forced to admit the necessity of an agreement acceptable to Irish nationalist opinion by breaking their power of veto. This may well have been a tactical error. Had the Liberals included cast-iron concessions in the original home rule bill, it is possible that Ulster Unionist opposition might have been divided, if not internally at least from broad swathes of sympathetic opinion in Great Britain. Instead Irish Unionists were able to concentrate agitation against an apparently extreme home rule bill determined to steamroll all opposition.

British and Irish unionists denied the right of impoverished, backward Catholic Ireland to insist upon home rule at the expense of imperial unity and the rights of protestantism and property in Ireland. However, in an increasingly democratic age, the mass resistance of Ulster—based widely on all

3 Bonar Law, leader of the Conservative Party, inspects the Ulster Volunteer Force, July 1914. His Majesty's Loyal Opposition supported armed resistance in Ulster to an Act of Parliament

classes of the Protestant community: farmer, worker, bour-geoisie, and gentry—was the key to defeating home rule. By default, Ulster self-determination emerged as the key ques-tion. There can be no doubting the furious and excellently organized Ulster Unionist opposition to home rule for Ireland.

For example, on 23 September 1911 a 'monster' meeting attended by 100,000 was held at Craigavon on the shores of Belfast Lough. Carson's speech made no bones of Unionist strategy: 'We must be prepared in the event of a Home Rule Bill passing, to take such measures as will enable us to carry on the government of those districts of which we have con-trol. We must be prepared, the morning Home Rule passes, ourselves to become responsible for the government of the Protestant province of Ulster.' British Tories, smarting from defeat and horrified at an assault on the integrity of the kingdom and empire, committed themselves to support Irish unionism's resistance.

In September 1912, 250,000 Unionists signed their names to a written declaration called the Solemn League and Covenant:

Being convinced in our consciences that Home Rule would be disastrous to the material well-being of Ulster as well as the whole of Ireland, subversive of our civil and religious free-dom, destructive of our citizenship, and perilous to the unity of the Empire [we] do hereby pledge ourselves ... to stand by one another in defending for ourselves and our children our cherished position of equal citizenship in the United Kingdom and in using all means which may be found

necessary to defeat the present conspiracy to set up a Home
Rule Parliament.

The following January the Ulster Volunteer Force (UVF), a
formidable political army staffed by the militarily experi-
enced gentry, gave credence to Unionist bravado. In April
1914 the UVF imported 25,000 rifles and three million
rounds of ammunition and by May Unionists were in a position to mobilize 23,000 men in defence of a provisional
Unionist government of the nine counties of Ulster. The provisional government met for the first time in July 1914.
There was much British sympathy for the Ulster cause in
Britain, particularly in the army. The Liberal prime minister,
Asquith, gloomily acknowledged that should he attempt to
use the military against the UVF, 'the instrument would
break' in his hands.

Nevertheless, there were risks inherent in such militarism.
Would the UVF really march out against the British army?
Many of its commanders were sure it would not, and had it
done so its rapid annihilation was a certainty. Would an
Ulster provisional government really have been able to rule
smoothly? In a province where almost half the population
was Catholic, and where the opposition Irish Nationalist
Volunteers enjoyed its densest support amongst nationalists,
this appears equally unlikely. Ulster Unionist strategy
appeared to be drifting towards a cataclysmic confrontation
with law and order, in which one can surmise that crucial
British sympathy would have melted way.

As part of an all-Irish alliance of the Protestant interest

against the claims of Catholic-nationalist democracy, Ulster Unionists until late in the day hoped to maintain a united Ireland represented directly at the United Kingdom parliament. With justice unionists can and have claimed that it was not they who partitioned Ireland, but Irish separatists. The rigour of Ulster Unionist opposition to going under a Dublin parliament forced the compromise of partition—it was not their ideal outcome. Even this may have been lost had events not gone their way.

Partition, thus, was a compromise around which both sides warily circled, well aware of the agonizing delicacy of their position. When the idea was first floated, in August 1911, Carson countered with a proposal that he knew to be unacceptable to the government: that the entire nine-county province of Ulster be separated. Asquith rejected the idea, as he still hoped to pass an unmitigated home rule act before opening serious negotiations with Ulster's unionists. Partition, however, was now on the agenda. David Lloyd George and his aide, Winston Churchill, presented the issue of exclusion of the northern counties from the home rule bill to the cabinet in February 1912. Later that year, the principal advocate of home rule, John Redmond, finally acquiesced to the proposal that Ulster counties should be permitted to opt out of home rule on an individual basis for a period of six years. The unionists rejected this as a mere 'stay of execution'. A conference to resolve the conflict was convened in July 1914 but reached an impasse. Thus home rule was due to become law without amendment. At this point World War One intervened.

Impact of the Great War

Given a German victory in the First World War it is likely that Ireland would have been severed from the United Kingdom *in toto,* just as the Allies dismembered the Austro-Hungarian and German empires. As the Sudeten Germans got short shrift, so too would have Ulster Protestants. As it happened, the First World War turned events much in unionism's favour. The Liberals, faced with unprecedented mutinies in the British army and a disastrous rift in British political opinion, had already concluded that Ulster could not be coerced. The pause imposed by the Great War meant that both sides could pull back from the brink and, in this context, a compromise could be agreed without fear of events escalating beyond control.

While the Great War pulled constitutional unionism back from the brink, it had the contrary effect on constitutional nationalism. Irish nationalism, well aware of its diminishing independent strength within the United Kingdom as the Irish population steadily declined, had long believed that its aspirations for an all-Ireland solution could only be realized by its allying itself to the coercive power of the British state. Only Britain had the wherewithal to overawe the unionist democracy in Ulster and the unionist ascendancy elsewhere in Ireland (a not insignificant 10 per cent of the population). The psychological cost had been high, however. Irish nationalist politicians had to mould themselves to the Catholic, romantic, rural, and anti-modern aspirations of their electorate. Equally, however, they had to play the supplicant in

England, allying themselves to liberalism, complete with its uncongenial enthusiasms for capitalism, imperialism, and secularism.

Playing the parliamentary game with little apparent success for thirty years from the welding together of the liberal–nationalist alliance in 1886, lacked the drama and uncomplicated glamour of nationalist mythology. The strains were evident in the revolution in Irish culture in the 1890s and 1900s, when a spurious neo-Gaelicism became the emblem of commitment to the nation. Seamy compromise with British political interests became increasingly repellent to articulate Irish Catholic opinion. Building the Catholic Gaelic utopia without external constraint loomed ever larger as the priority. The failure of constitutional nationalism to secure a settlement with unionist opinion, despite its apparent readiness to barter the essentials of nationalist aspirations, prepared a climate propitious for a revolution in nationalist psychology.

The rise of republicanism

In Easter 1916 a brief republican attempt at *coup d'état* devastated the centre of Dublin and following the execution of sixteen of its leaders, added to the succession of Irish martyrs at the hands of British oppression. This flourish brought to a head the purist riposte to constitutional nationalism's equivocation. The growing burdens of the First World War, a conflict in which few Irish nationalists felt much commitment, accelerated the process of disillusionment. The threat of conscription in 1918 was perhaps the last straw. In the post-armistice 1918 election, Irish nationalism swung massively if not completely behind the Sinn Féin (Ourselves Alone) party. Catholic Ireland repudiated further parleying with the British political system from within and, in effect, gave up on conciliating Irish unionist opinion. Refusing to take their seats at Westminster, the Sinn Féin MPs convened at the Mansion House in Dublin in early 1919 as the new parliament of the Irish Republic, Dáil Éireann.

Partition

This was a huge boon to Ulster Unionism, a fact clear to Catholic opinion in Ulster which was much the most unwilling to tread the Sinn Féin path. As abstention and civil disobedience in the south escalated into a war of sorts, Ulster Unionism sat pretty. Its British allies were secure in the cabinet, and Ulster's sterling war service contrasted favourably to the outright subversion of Republican rebels. The 1920 Government of Ireland Act awarded six counties—Antrim, Down, Armagh, Fermanagh, Derry, and Tyrone—to a parliament to sit in Belfast under the United Kingdom parliament but virtually severed from Dublin. This was a catastrophe for nationalists in the new state of Northern Ireland. Only a few years previously, the worst-case scenario was a four-county opt-out (Antrim, Down, Armagh, Derry), perhaps only for a limited period, and administered directly

by a Westminster parliament where Irish nationalist representations would have provided a powerful voice in their
favour. They were the victims of southern nationalism's
exhaustion with compromise, but it is perhaps little surprise
that they began to see their own salvation in an extremist
repudiation of the new state's legitimacy and a toleration for
armed revolt.

Was partition meant to be absolute and indefinite? The
Government of Ireland Act contained a clause that foresaw the
establishment of a Council of Ireland to harmonize and
ultimately unify the island under 'a parliament for the whole
of Ireland'. James Craig (later Lord Craigavon), Northern
Ireland's first prime minister, connived in the council's
demise, but did send out signals that 'Ulster might be wooed
by sympathetic understanding—she can never be coerced'.
Basil Brooke (later Lord Brookeborough), who succeeded
Craigavon, had as a minister seriously considered agreeing
to Irish unity if this would bring the south of Ireland into
the war against Nazi Germany. Terence O'Neill, Brookeborough's successor, expressed the opinion after his retire-
ment that Irish unity was inevitable, if not in his lifetime.

This suggests certain insecurity about the long-term viabil-
ity of the northern statelet, hardly hallowed by long tradition
and still seen by most of the British Isles (including most
unionists) as inherently 'Irish'. Ulster Unionists were well
aware of British indifference to Northern Ireland's fate relative to geopolitical concerns. Twice, in 1921 and in the early
years of the Second World War, Britain put pressure on the
Northern Ireland government to reach a *modus vivendi* with

Dublin for the greater good of the empire. It also reflected the sense that, despite the careful carving of the border to ensure a safe unionist majority, the Catholic minority was encroaching. Catholics had a birth rate approximately double that of the Protestant population. Official census figures, however, showed that between 1937 and 1961 the Catholic population of the province remained virtually static: 33.5 per cent in 1937, 34.9 per cent in 1961. During this period, Catholic emigration represented 21 per cent of the Catholic population, whilst Protestant emigration represented only 8 per cent of the Protestant population. Only differences in economic opportunity maintained the status quo. On this bare fact rested many unionist practices during the years of home rule in Northern Ireland.

The Troubles of the early 1920s

One possible solution was to wean the Catholic minority, or a section of it, from its truculent adherence to Irish nationalism. 'From the outset let us see that the Catholic minority have nothing to fear from the Protestant majority,' said Lord Carson when relinquishing his leadership of the Ulster Unionist movement in 1921. 'Let us take care to win all that is best among those who have been opposed to us in the past. While maintaining intact our own religion let us give the same rights to the religion of our neighbours.' The minority were not to be so easily placated, however. Ulster's Catholics hoped to make home rule in Northern Ireland unworkable, just as Ulster Unionists had made all-Ireland home rule unworkable. They enjoyed few of their advantages, however. As a subaltern class, they could not rely upon gentry and the business elite to finance and officer militant resistance. Their putative leaders—the republican warlords of southern Ireland—accorded their cause low priority and were too weak militarily to lend much substantial aid. And while Ulster Unionism's leadership had restrained rank-and-file militancy in 1912–14, for fear of precipitating a conflagration fatal to their battle for opinion in Great Britain, they could now unleash it under the pretext of defeating armed subversion and to defend an established fact. IRA activity sparked mass expulsions of Catholic disloyalists from major workplaces and residential centres.

Overall, the violence in Ulster following partition, a bloody front in the Anglo-Irish War, was almost as much against Protestants as Catholics; 157 Protestants died in the two years up to July 1922, and 37 members of the security forces, compared to 257 Catholics. But the orgy of violence in 1922, which followed the treaty between Britain and elements of the Sinn Féin leadership, proved much more one-sided; Catholics were battered into submission. More people died in Belfast during three months of violence in 1922 than in the whole two years following the formation of the state. A substantial majority of the 232 victims were Catholic, and 11,000 were made jobless and 23,000 homeless. Over 4,500 Catholic-owned shops and businesses were burned, looted, or wrecked. Property worth £3 million was destroyed.

Human rights

The Special Powers Act (SPA) of 1922 gave the security forces in Northern Ireland powers to arrest without warrant, detain without trial, search homes without warrants, prohibit meetings and processions, and hang and whip offenders. It was not usually applied with full rigour, but became an embarrassment when, in April 1963, J. Voster, South African minister of justice, whilst introducing a new coercion bill quipped that he 'would be willing to exchange all the legislation of that sort for one clause of the Northern Ireland Special Powers Act'. In fact the SPA provided similar powers to those retained by the Republic of Ireland. Its provision for imprisonment without trial—internment—was activated between 1971 and 1975, when 2,158 were interned.

The SPA was repealed in 1973 to be replaced by the Emergency Powers Act (EPA). Scheduled (i.e. paramilitary) offences were dealt with by juryless Diplock courts, for fear of partisan or intimidated juries returning perverse judgements. There is no evidence that Diplock courts are particularly prone to miscarriages of justice. The EPA reversed the burden of proof on bail applications and made easier the admission of uncorroborated confession statements. Fewer than about 75 per cent arrested under the EPA were charged—the aim was usually to harass and gather intelligence. Those lifted were taken to holding centres, notably Castlereagh, near Belfast, where they could be held without charge for seven days, for conveyer-belt interrogation. Solicitors were not permitted to be present during interview. Allegations of brutality were widespread, and as the RUC investigated complaints themselves, there was little faith that complaints would be fairly considered.

In 1974 the Prevention of Terrorism (Temporary Provisions) Act was passed following IRA bombs in Great Britain itself. It extended aspects of emergency legislation throughout the United Kingdom. Police were empowered to hold anyone suspected of terrorism for up to 48 hours, and a further five days with the permission of the home secretary. Citizens of Northern Ireland could be excluded from travelling to mainland Britain.

Initially CS (tear) gas was used to disperse crowds, but this proved hard to control, drifting towards security-force lines and into residential areas. Along with water cannon, it created unwelcome images of the battlefield for international television. The standard for riot control from 1973 was the rubber and then the plastic bullet. 124,829 plastic bullets had been fired by the end of 1998, killing 17 people, 12 of whom were children.

In 1973 a standing advisory commission on human rights was established, one of the first such bodies of its kind in the world. Successive governments largely ignored it. Following the Good Friday Agreement, an enormous range of unelected bodies was appointed to wrestle with human-rights issues. These included an independent police ombudsman's office, a criminal cases review commission, a victims' commission, a human rights commission, a location of victims' remains commission, a second Bloody Sunday inquiry, a parades commission, an international commission on decommissioning, a sentence review commission, an equality commission, and an independent commission on policing.

Despite this, the Troubles have produced a ratchet shift in attitudes, and much 'emergency' legislation is likely to be made a permanent feature of the legislative framework of society.

Ulster Unionism consolidates

The state was buttressed by the paramilitary organization of Protestant males into the Ulster Special Constabulary, a reborn UVF now enjoying the financial and moral backing of the British state. Catholic resistance was beaten back and, following Britain's successful playing on divisions with republican opinion in the 1921 treaty negotiations, collapsed as its southern Irish sponsors dissolved into the feuding factions of civil war. The cost had been high in casualties, however, and the unionist state was confronted from the outset with a rebellious, intransigent Catholic minority.

Unionists were loath to rely upon Britain as a counterweight to Catholic hostility. British prime minister Lloyd George, his eyes fixed upon cutting a deal with moderates in the nationalist leadership in the south, had canvassed with Craig (the north's prime minister) the idea of Northern Ireland retaining its autonomy but going under a Dublin parliament itself subordinate to the crown. Craig indignantly rejected this proposal, but the looming Boundary Commission, which threatened to readjust the border perhaps to the disadvantage of the north, stretched out the agony of Ulster Unionist uncertainty. Only in 1926 was the Boundary Commission wound up with the border left as it was. As unionists exulted, nationalists finally admitted that the Northern Ireland state would not merely be a passing phase. Their leader, Joe Devlin, now Nationalist MP for West Belfast, entered the Northern Ireland House of Commons in April 1925. In January 1926 he appealed to his fellow Nationalist

MPs to take their seats: 'He . . . declared that the reasons had disappeared why they should remain out of [Parliament]. It was their business . . . to recognise the Northern Parliament in the interests of democracy.'

Despite this, unionists took two fundamental lessons from the foundation of Northern Ireland. First, that Catholics were irretrievably opposed to the very existence of the state and, second, that Britain did not see Northern Ireland as a unit enjoying inalienable self-determination, but merely as a compromise solution, perhaps temporary, of a knotty problem. Partition was a solution that could be unmade at Britain's will. Stormont became a bulwark against nationalist conniving and British treachery. This was expressed well by an Ulster Unionist resolution issued in 1936:

> The cry 'back to Westminster' is a subtle move fraught with great danger. Had we refused to accept a Parliament for Northern Ireland and remained at Westminster there can be little doubt that by now we would be either inside the Free State [southern Ireland] or fighting desperately against incorporation. Northern Ireland without a Parliament of her own would be a standing temptation to certain British politicians to make a bid for a final settlement with Irish Republicans.

The conclusions drawn here became meshed in the unionist mind. Catholics had to be prevented from insinuating themselves into the apparatus of the state. Their loyalty would never be anything more than conditional, temporary, and probably insincere. Over one third of the population was to be regarded as a permanent threat.

Conclusion

From the sixteenth century, Ireland's separate Gaelic society was steadily destroyed. Ireland modernized under British direction. That Ireland's ruling elite owed its position to conquest was not unusual for early modern Europe. It was the coincidence of conquest with religious schism that prevented the emergence of a nation state uniting all classes. For the conquered Irish, adherence to Roman Catholicism provided consolation and hope for profane benefit should the true religion be restored in Britain. Protestantism served as a mark of superiority for the conquerors, both morally justifying their dominance and preventing dispersal of their privileges.

The United Irishmen of the 1790s failed to overcome these religious and caste antagonisms, which instead in the nineteenth century reconfigured around rival national allegiances. Religious identity was reworked, not weakened, by new psychologies of national fellow-feeling generated by the mobility and literacy of Ireland's market economy. The Protestant culture of Great Britain worked against the satisfaction of Irish nationalism within the United Kingdom. But the alternative of separation was certain to meet the opposition of Protestant Ulster. As an entire society of all classes, it proved much more able to adapt to the rise of democratic self-determination than the Protestant elite spread thinly throughout the rest of Ireland.

The democracy Ulster Unionism came to espouse was of a certain type, however. For long it had supported its case primarily on the inability of Catholic Ireland to govern fairly. Support for parallel self-determination of both Irish national groups came late and was only half-formed even by the time of Partition, enacted by Britain upon this principle. Unionist anti-catholicism, now primarily directed against a large internal minority, fused with an intolerant majoritarian democracy. Northern Ireland's Catholics, meanwhile, resented the sacrifice of their identity to political expediency by both Ulster Unionism and Irish separatism. Fearing absorption, they set out to ignore as best they could the structures of the new state.

2

Home Rule in Ulster:
Stormont's Record

Northern Ireland's purpose-built parliament building at Stormont, near Belfast, was opened in 1932. Its neoclassical grandeur was overblown for the limited powers and importance of the statelet it represented. It reflected the desire of the Unionist establishment to present a stolid confidence to the world. The reality was very different.

Threats to Ulster Unionism

During the crucial years of Northern Ireland's establishment, British pressure for a compromise with southern nationalists had only been kept at bay by the regimenting of Ulster's Protestants. This united front had to be maintained in the face of all other issues that might tend to fragment the alliance. Were the Union to appear consolidated, perhaps because Ulster Catholics were downplaying their essential nationalism, it was feared that Protestants would look to sectional interests rather than remain mobilized for the Union. Above all it was anticipated that class interests would lead a

4 The Stormont Building, with a statue of Lord Carson in the foreground. Despite the grandeur of Northern Ireland's parliament, it administered a population no larger than an average English county

section of Protestant workers to turn to the Labour cause. It must be emphasized that Unionists did not believe that Protestant workers could be tempted into an all-Ireland settlement, socialist or otherwise. All-Ireland socialism had no appeal for Protestant workers, nor was their loyalty to the Union based upon petty bribes thrown their way by the Unionist elite. Rather, it was feared that Protestant workers, believing the constitution was secure, would vote for Labour representatives on day-to-day issues.

This could have two disastrous consequences from a Unionist point of view. Either British political opinion would come to believe that Ulster Unionism was breaking apart, and take the opportunity to sell out their interests for a deal with all-Ireland nationalism. This seemed possible more than once, as when Chamberlain strove to appease Eamon De Valera, the hard-line premier of southern Ireland, in the late 1930s and early 1940s. A second possibility was the splitting of the Protestant vote, the fall from power of the Ulster Unionist party, and the coming to power of an alternative government in Northern Ireland. In a parliamentary democracy, of course, changes of government are not unusual. Unionists, however, could not afford one. Facing an approaching election in 1929, the *Belfast News-Letter* warned its readers that 'The issue is whether a Unionist Government shall continue to control affairs, safeguard the interest, and help to shape the destination of Northern Ireland, or whether the task is to be entrusted to some fortuitous combination of Nationalists, Socialists, and Independents'.

A non-Unionist government would not be answerable for its actions until the next general election. Thus buffered from the natural Unionist majority in Northern Ireland, and driven by ill-concealed ideological priorities (the Northern Ireland Labour Party (NILP) did not formally accept the permanence of the state until 1949), such a government might by instalments negotiate an all-Ireland settlement.

Might Unionists have lost control of Northern Ireland?

This scenario may appear implausible, but in fact Unionists had a surprisingly small number of absolutely secure seats in the Northern Ireland parliament. Losing an election was a real possibility.

Certainly, it was very unlikely that such an alternative government could win an election on a platform opposing the Union. But it was conceivable that an alliance of Unionist labourists and Catholic representatives could come to power on a limited domestic-reform programme. Once in power, however, such an unholy alliance of crypto-nationalists and socialists might be tempted to change the rules of the electoral game, excluding the Unionists from power indefinitely. As the future Ulster Unionist leader, Harry West argued as late as 1969, 'If the Unionist Government ever goes out of power it will never get back in again. The opposition will so manipulate things that it will be impossible for the Unionist Party ever to return to power.'

Of the 52 single-member seats and four Queen's University seats that made up the Northern Ireland House of Commons between 1929 and 1972, a total of 25 fell from Unionist control at least once. A further seven were at least once held on to with less than 51 per cent of the vote, another six with between 51 and 55 per cent. Broadly defined, thus, no less than 38 seats, almost 68 per cent of the total, were at one time or another lost to the Unionist party or marginal.

Of course, all this was potential. When Unionists registered losses they often had gains elsewhere as compensation. Nor was the opposition united: nationalists, socialists, and independent unionists never effectively coordinated efforts nor even peaked simultaneously. There was a regular core of about ten Nationalist and two Labour seats; thus the natural Unionist complement was 40. That this was only achieved in 1921 indicates the unsteadiness of the Unionist bloc. However, by seeing off various challenges sequentially, Ulster Unionist representation generally oscillated comfortably in the upper 30s. It never, after the abolition of proportional representation in 1929, fell below 34 seats.

Nevertheless, 'nightmare' scenarios were distinctly imaginable. The core of instability was Belfast; it was a real possibility that the Ulster Unionist regular complement of 12 or so of the 16 seats could tumble to half that. The threat here was from Labour and populist unionist candidates. Of the 16 single-member seats in Belfast, contested 11 times between 1929 and 1969, no fewer than 10 were lost to the Unionist party at least once. In two seats Unionists held on with a minority of the poll; in another two they were squeezed to less than 55 per cent. Only Cromac and Windsor appeared really solid. The loss of 14 out of 16 rocky seats in Belfast was a catastrophe waiting to happen.

The four Queen's University seats were never reliable, and indeed Unionists in due course lost two. The broad swathe of Antrim, Down, and Armagh was generally immune to socialist siren calls, but Presbyterian, tenant right, populist, and, as Belfast's middle-class dormitories swelled, Liberal Unionist

Unionist plans for a united Ireland?

Terence O'Neill, Liberal Unionist Prime Minister of Northern Ireland, defied the cold war between north and south in January 1964 when he met the Irish Republic's Taoiseach (PM), Sean Lemass. In February the following year he made the return visit, this time with wives present, to Dublin. Years later, in 1973, Sean Lemass's widow, Kathleen, made a remarkable claim about this meeting:

> Sean explained to me that they [O'Neill and Lemass] wanted to convey the impression to the outside world that the talks were just about routine matters. In fact, both men wanted to see Ireland united. Their idea was to have several meetings at various levels between Government officials so that co-operation would begin, eventually leading to Irish unity. Very few people have known until this day that both of those men wanted the unification of Ireland and I am convinced they could have achieved it.

That a straightforward reunification in the short term was discussed is very unlikely. However, O'Neill, who had been raised in England, considered himself as Anglo-Irish, not Ulster Protestant. He was akin to the southern Irish Protestants of the nineteenth century, in that he was 'romantically involved with Ireland', believing that 'London is the capital of the British Isles and that the Monarch is the Head of your State.'

In 1969 he predicted:

> ... regional parliaments all over Britain having a federal relationship with Westminster. When that is established I think

> it is possible that the South of Ireland Parliament will have an association with this federation . . . the kind of association that would mean the British Isles becoming the British Isles again.
>
> Is there an echo of this in the (Unionist) provision in the Belfast Good Friday Agreement for a British-Irish Council?
>
> After his resignation as prime minister, O'Neill revealed that 'he was sure that one day, there would be a united Ireland', though not in his lifetime. Unionist pessimism about the future of the Union is not all that uncommon. We hear inklings of it over the years in stray statements from leaders as diverse as Lord Craigavon, Bill Craig, and even Ian Paisley. Privately many wonder how they might make a future united Ireland more amenable to themselves. Until and if a Catholic nationalist majority in Northern Ireland emerges, however, such musings are likely to remain carefully concealed.

candidates all had their appeal. It was by no means paranoid to imagine the loss of two or three of the Ulster Unionist Party's regular phalanx of 15 or so MPs from the inner counties.

Thus a collapse in Belfast and mere slippage elsewhere could easily whittle the Unionist domination of 40 MPs against 12 opposition MPs down to 30 Unionist against 22 opposition. This made the outer counties—Derry, Fermanagh, and Tyrone—absolutely crucial.

A purely Catholic–nationalist challenge, if unimpeded and coordinated, could certainly snatch four of the seven Unionist seats in Derry, Fermanagh, and Tyrone. Fermanagh was dangerously balanced. Both Enniskillen and Lisnaskea were vulnerable, if strongly challenged as they were in the late 1960s, when Unionists fell below 51 per cent of the vote. Londonderry South was firmly Unionist, Foyle and Mid firmly Nationalist, but North and City were precarious; in City the Unionist candidate scraped home with 39.4 per cent in 1969, in North only a shade over 50 per cent. Tyrone returned two Unionists to three Nationalists, but both Ulster Unionist candidates won less than 55 per cent of the vote in 1969.

A realistic scenario of Unionists shedding six seats in Belfast and losing two Queen's seats, another two in the heartland, and four in the border areas, would convert a putative Unionist majority of 40 seats against 12 into a deadlocked Commons of 26 for the government, 26 against. There was plenty of scope for worse than this. The massive population advantage enjoyed by Unionists, and the comfortable Ulster Unionist majorities regularly returned to Stormont hid a frightening electoral precariousness.

Electoral discrimination

In an uncertain world, Unionists had little alternative but to contemplate the worst-case scenario. Their priority, thus, was to keep the Union as the one burning issue. Elections were held at the prime minister's discretion, always when the Union seemed most at risk, serving the dual function of delivering a message to Britain and maintaining the Unionist alliance on an eternal war footing. Unionists clarified the electoral system by abolishing proportional representation in 1929. This weakened minority parties, particularly Labour, and consolidated the Unionist/Nationalist rift. Representation for Labour, independent unionists, and other groups, fell from eight seats in 1925 to four in 1929, although their share of the vote increased.

In common with Great Britain, the Northern Ireland local government electorate was based upon a ratepayer's franchise. But when this was abolished in Britain after the Second World War, Stormont elected to retain it. Protestants made up the majority of the 250,000 thus deprived of local government vote, but Catholics, being lower down the socioeconomic scale and thus less likely to pay rates, were disproportionately outside the franchise. Only in one local authority—Armagh Urban District—was Unionist control so precarious that it could be overturned by a simple change in the franchise.

The importance to Unionists of the ratepayer's franchise was that it locked in the principle that those who paid the most rates were entitled to the biggest say in the conduct of local government. Local government boundaries were required by law to be based on regard for rateable value (under the Towns Improvement (Ireland) Act 1854). If wards were to reflect the level of rates paid rather than population, then small but relatively wealthy areas were entitled to return as many councillors as large but relatively poor areas. Richer areas were disproportionately Unionist.

The political results of this principle were starkly revealed in the 1923 redrawing of many local government constituency boundaries to reflect changing patterns of wealth. Nationalist councils fell in great number to Unionist control. Similar re-jigs, all perfectly legitimate as attempts to equalize the rateable values of local government constituencies, won or consolidated for unionism Omagh Urban District in 1935, Derry County Borough in 1936, Armagh Urban District in 1946, and Fermanagh in 1966. Perhaps one fifth of Catholics lived under gerrymandered constituencies.

Such considerations were vital to Unionists to the bitter end, and explain their furious and disastrous resistance to the civil rights demand of 'one man one vote'. The Stormont cabinet was well aware of the existence of anomalies in electoral districts, and, in 1964, even resisted a full census with questions on religion for fear of throwing 'into relief difficult political questions of redistribution'. It was feared that the concession of universal suffrage in local government would be 'traitorous to the loyalists of Tyrone, Fermanagh, Londonderry and Armagh' (Young Unionist resolution, April 1969). Unionists felt that, as long as they stuck to the original 'bargain' implicit in devolution, they had a right to defend their political interests. Tom Lyons, a hard-liner, in 1968 swore against giving even 'a quarter of an inch' on one man one vote: 'We took over in 1921 under certain conditions. The principles were all laid down and we have abided by them very accurately. Like most parliaments, we like to protect our own authority, and we propose to do so by refusing to touch one man one vote.' John Dobson, another Unionist MP, agreed: 'The main argument is that one should make a change to benefit one's political opponents. I can't see any Government at Westminster doing that.'

Control of local government authorities gave Unionists a micro-management of the Stormont constituencies. The organizational development of opposition parties was retarded with so few outlets in representative assemblies. Gerrymandering ensured that the symbolic Unionist integrity of the six counties was maintained. In British eyes at least, a nominal Unionist majority in Northern Ireland would be much discounted if Derry City, Fermanagh, and Tyrone fell into Nationalist hands. Gerrymandering had the further advantage of maintaining important sources of patronage in Unionist hands. Excessive population mobility always threatened to undermine Unionist majorities, and it became a priority to corral Catholic (and Labour) voters into well-defined constituencies. Thus a careful eye was kept on local-authority housing to ensure that Catholic and Protestant populations did not bleed into each other, for fear of anti-Unionist tactical voting on the part of Catholics and Labour-minded Protestants.

Economic discrimination

As a consequence, however, there was pressure to maintain the relative wealth disparities of Catholic and Protestant districts, or else the entire delicate framework would collapse. There were structural factors that suppressed overall Catholic wealth and employment relative to Protestant: large

Catholic family size, their concentration in peripheral areas west of the River Bann, and relatively poor standards of education in Catholic-run schools that enjoyed lower levels of state subsidy. However, the delicate balance of local government constituencies could be upset by shifts in very local employment, and there was sometimes deliberate discrimination at this level.

The inter-war period was one of limited material resources, both north and south of the border. In this environment, rhetoric was a cheap resource often tapped. Southern Irish nationalism shed much of its remaining tradition of secularism, and the politicians of Independent Ireland bowed to the trinity of catholicism, Gaelicism, and autarchy (the latter two rather lacking as concrete manifestation). Unionist fears that home rule in Ireland would mean Rome rule often appeared amply justified by an extraordinary identification of state and society with a strident Roman catholicism. The Irish premier, de Valera, could blithely declare in 1935 that Ireland was 'a Catholic nation'.

Much Unionist rhetoric simply echoed such sectarian triumphalism, but at least the southern Protestant minority were sufficiently non-threatening and socially privileged to suffer more from condescension that outright persecution. Unionist minister Basil Brooke in 1933 admitted that Protestants in the Free State might well get a 'square deal', but this was because they were a declining minority of no threat to the state. Catholics in Northern Ireland, on the other hand, 'were increasing', 'ninety-seven per cent . . . disruptive and disloyal' and thus he advised employers 'Do not employ

Roman Catholics where they could get good Protestants to take their place.'

As late as 1957, formal arrangements were made with Du Pont, an American multinational operating in Derry, to ensure that the personnel manager was a Unionist Party nominee and that a 'proportionate' number of Protestants be hired.*

In housing, there was the same attention to detail. Overall, Catholics got roughly the percentage of public housing due to them. But extraordinary attention was paid to their placing, again so as not to upset constituencies. In 1964 the Unionist chairman of Enniskillen Housing Committee, George Elliott, argued that 'it is only common-sense, after all, that a Unionist Council is not going to put people into houses who are going to vote against them at the next election.' Unionists were ever watchful of their electoral position. They resented that the Housing Trust, a centrally organized bureaucracy free of sectarian taint, which allocated as many houses as did the local authorities, had the power to upset this position. A statement from the Middle Liberties Unionist Association in Derry was handed to a Twelfth platform in 1967 which read:

> Discrimination against Protestants in Middle Liberties, where you are now meeting. The Northern Ireland Housing Trust (Unionist Government appointed) has made the following

---

* Cabinet Conclusions, 19 November 1957, Public Records Office of Northern Ireland (PRONI) CAB/4/1023/14, p.4.

allocations in the new estate to date—Roman Catholics 255, Protestants 23. As a result the seat was thrown away at the last Rural District Council election to non-Unionists. What do you really think of this? Please tell the crowd.

Economy

Northern Ireland's economy was based upon agriculture, textiles, and engineering. The jewel in the crown was Harland & Wolff shipyard, the largest in the world, where the *Titanic* was built. Anti-home rule propaganda emphasized north-east Ulster's successful industrial revolution in contrast to the rest of Ireland, but ironically the foundation of the new state coincided with a profound crisis in its rather narrow base of industries. The Depression hit Northern Ireland hard, with rates of employment approaching 25 per cent. The Stormont government strove to maintain Protestant employment, but its success in attracting an increasing contribution from Britain to support welfare and development meant that Catholics benefited also. Between 1926 and 1961 the number of Catholics in Northern Ireland increased by 18 per cent, while total population increase was 13 per cent; over the same period the Catholic population of the south declined by almost 3 per cent.

The Second World War briefly restored the fortunes of traditional industries, but in the post-war period Northern Ireland's unemployment was some 5 per cent higher than in Great Britain. The province was burdened with high transport and energy costs, without sufficiently compensating low wages. By 1969 only 183,000 people were still working in manufacturing in Northern Ireland, compared with 303,000 at the end of the war. New investment, particularly in synthetic fibres—Du Pont, Courtaulds, ICI, and Enkelon amongst others—did something to arrest the decline. Overall, the economy diversified and grew, but the publicly subsidized sector (including Harland & Wolff) expanded enormously—from 22.5 per cent of the manufacturing workforce in 1961 to 44.9 per cent in 1972.

This accelerated during the Troubles. From £100 million in 1968 and £181 million in 1972, the bill for the British state shot to £1 billion in 1980, £2 billion in 1990, and around £3.5 billion a decade later. In the 1980s Northern Ireland had the most substantial health and education provision in the UK, while also having the highest level of unemployment and the lowest level of income. Catholics, perhaps due to their historic concentration in areas of high unemployment and low grades within jobs, were disproportionately affected. Protestants enjoyed almost all the economic advantages of 20,000 well-paid jobs (about 10 per cent of total Protestant employment) connected to the security forces.

Nevertheless, in 1990 standards of living were still around 40 per cent higher in the north than in the Republic of Ireland. Consumer spending per head in the north was one third above the southern level, government spending per head on public services two thirds higher This was a formidable argument against Irish unity.

The picture changed in the 1990s as the Republic of Ireland enjoyed an extraordinary boom. The Irish economy became the fastest growing in Europe. Unemployment fell and incomes rose by 44 per cent over the period of the peace process. Economic growth ran at over 7 per cent per annum from the mid-1990s. Northern Ireland has enjoyed less spectacular success, but has seen prosperity buttressed by funding from the United States and the European Union to support the peace process. The two economies have converged somewhat, though Northern Ireland's greater dependence on resources from the rest of the United Kingdom economy, and the Republic's continuing social inequality and pockets of poverty, means that there may be a case for north–south cooperation, but hardly yet for integration.

In regional economic policy local discrimination designed to maintain the balance of constituencies meshed with Stormont-led schemes. In the inter-war years, this amounted to little more than 'distributing the bones', as Craigavon, Northern Ireland's prime minister, called it, i.e. small-scale hand outs to loyal local authorities. By the 1960s, however, large-scale economic plans were afoot. Notably, the 'new city', Craigavon (provocatively named after Northern Ireland's first prime minister), was intended to absorb Portadown and Lurgan in County Armagh. This raised Unionist fears that Catholic immigrants would flood from counties Fermanagh and Tyrone, creating a Nationalist majority in County Armagh, and losing Unionist seats. The city's planner, Geoffrey Copcutt, some years later confirmed to *The Times* that 'during the planning of the city . . . he was told by a source close to the Northern Ireland Cabinet that the Ulster Government would not countenance any scheme that would upset the voting balance between Protestants and Roman Catholics in the area'. Indeed, a policy of 'selective intake' was adopted to ensure that 'the proportions of families in the different community groupings will be similar to that of the Province as a whole' (Second Report on the New City). Urban redevelopment was clearly being manipulated so as not to upset the communal balance of power.

Derry City

The most striking focus of all these discontents was Derry/Londonderry. Its gerrymandering, again employing the 'rateable value' defence, was stark. In a gerrymander in 1923 Unionists wrested control from Nationalists, an arrangement reinforced in the 1930s. A prominent Unionist MP, Edmund Warnock, recalled this as Derry led the way in the civil rights movement of 1968:

> If ever a community had a right to demonstrate against a denial of civil rights, Derry is the finest example. A Roman Catholic and Nationalist city has for three or four decades been administered (and none too fairly administered) by a Protestant and Unionist majority secured by a manipulation of the Ward boundaries for the sole purpose of retaining Unionist control.
>
> I was consulted by Sir James Craig [prime minister], Dawson Bates and R. D. Megaw at the time it was done. Craig thought that the fate of our constitution was on a knife-edge at the time and that, in the circumstances, it was defensible on the basis that the safety of the State was the supreme law.*

* Letter to Terence O'Neill included in Cabinet Conclusions, PRONI, 13 November 1968, CAB/4/1414/5.

Derry's City North Ward with an electorate of 5,000 returned eight Unionist seats; South Ward returned eight Nationalists, but had an electorate of 15,000. Waterside, with 5,000 electors, returned four Unionists. Thus a Nationalist majority of 5,000 resulted in a Unionist council of twelve Unionists to eight Nationalists.

A Unionist cabal in the city—infamous in the 1960s as 'the faceless men'—conspired to restrict Derry's economic growth for fear of upsetting the rate-based gerrymander: the city boundary was artificially restricted; Catholic public housing, when built, was packed into Nationalist wards; new industries and even Northern Ireland's second university, planned in 1965, were lobbied against. Dr Nixon, Unionist MP for North Down, pleaded with his colleagues in 1965: 'You cannot run away . . . from Derry City where the population is 60 per cent Nationalist and 34 per cent Unionist. You cannot maintain Ulster this way.'

Job discrimination

Fear of Catholic infiltration limited recruitment of Catholics to the higher echelons of the state, and little was done to encourage a conciliatory policy on the part of the political representatives. Throughout the Stormont era there was consistent and largely successful pressure from the Unionist grassroots to keep Catholics out of senior public employment positions. In 1933 the minister of labour (and future prime minister), J. M. Andrews, was positively

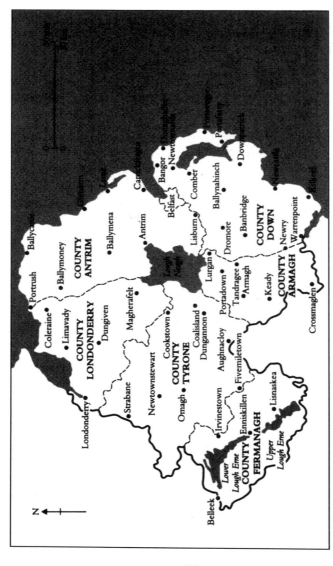

5 County map of Northern Ireland. The electoral geography of Northern Ireland was a Unionist obsession

defensive in assuring his supporters: 'Another allegation made against the Government and which was untrue, was that, of 31 porters at Stormont, 28 were Roman Catholics. I have investigated the matter, and I find that there are 30 Protestants, and only one Roman Catholic there temporarily.'

This anxiety continued into the 1960s. Noting the introduction of competitive examination into the civil service, Lieutenant-Colonel D. C. Liddle, vice-chairman of the Ulster Unionist Council, warned in January 1965 that unless young Unionists applied themselves to education 'in another ten or fifteen years' time we will have lost control of all the executive positions—Post Office, Civil Service and local government'. When, in 1966, a commission was established to oversee the development of the 'new city', potentially crucial in determining the sectarian electoral geography of Northern Ireland, only one of the nine members was Catholic. Few of the appointees had any relevant expertise and one government supporter judged it fit only 'for running a Unionist garden fete'.

Unionist leaders were complicit in the rousing of sectarian passions by their pointed demonization of the Nationalist and Catholic aspirations of the minority. In 1935 these passions ignited into fatal rioting. Folk memory of mass clearing of disloyal elements from workplaces and residential areas, and the response of IRA gunmen avenging if not entirely defending besieged Catholics, was refreshed.

Catholics, in their turn, barely recognized the state and waited sourly for 'the day' when they would be reunited with their southern brethren. (With their own newspapers, sports clubs, social venues, and Roman-Catholic-controlled education system, Ulster Catholics could if they chose turn their backs on the Northern Ireland state.) Nationalists and their allies could generally count on having 11 seats in the Commons out of 52. The reluctance of the anti-partitionists to appear to sanction the existence of the state militated against the creation of any durable Nationalist Party organization or machinery on a par with that of the Unionists. The parliamentary group tended to exist from election to election very much on an *ad hoc* basis, and was susceptible to the problems of disunity, and lack of any effective or dynamic leadership. Periodically Nationalists would quit Stormont with a flourish, only to return grumpily as Unionist government blithely continued.

Reform and 'revolution'

Northern Ireland had a good World War, consolidating its position as a defensive outpost for the United Kingdom and earning a grateful loyalty to the Unionist cause from a generation of British politicians. On the back of this, the province was able to participate in the welfare state, allowing the import of labourism at no political cost to the Unionist united front, and in 1949 the added bonus of the Ireland Act, which for the first time recognized Northern Ireland's right to self-determination.

This new dispensation was slowly to bring its own

problems, however. As the Ireland Act made Stormont, rather than the people of Northern Ireland consulted through referendum, the final arbiter, control of that assembly remained crucial and the party-state was perpetuated. The massive expansion of state largesses, moreover, complicated and brought to the fore Unionist tactics in the manipulation of electoral sectarian geography. A major attempt to impose the price of loyalty on Catholics for the benefits of the British welfare state was attempted in the 1950s. All civil-service and public-sector workers, even those digging ditches for the Forestry Commission as unemployment relief, were required to undergo the galling humiliation of swearing an oath to the monarch.

If this reflected a warding off of the long-term evil of a Catholic majority, short-term problems presented themselves with the disaffection of Protestant workers, who by the late 1950s were increasingly turning to the Northern Ireland Labour Party (NILP). Unionism faced the very real prospect of losing Belfast. In 1963 Terence O'Neill became prime minister with the brief of seeing off the Labour challenge. This he did, with surprising ease, by adopting a technocratic set of policies designed to attract British subventions for the renovation of the province's economic superstructure. O'Neill had wider ambitions than this, however. He sincerely hoped to break the mould of sectarian politics by detaching a section of Catholic opinion from weary nationalism.

O'Neill explained his policy in trademark patrician manner: 'I have been trying to . . . persuade Catholics in

Northern Ireland that they have a place within the United Kingdom. I have been succeeding, first with the professional class, and gradually with the artisans. I don't believe Catholics in Ulster want to be governed by the Republic of Ireland.' There was some basis for this: the post-war welfare state certainly gave Catholics a greater stake in the United Kingdom. Another Unionist MP, addressing a pro-O'Neill gathering, explained Terence O'Neill's rationale: given the birth rate of Catholics, unless some of their number could be won over 'the Unionists could exist only for another twenty years and [then] the boat would sink.' The *Belfast Telegraph* in 1969 commented that 'implicit in the O'Neill doctrine is the faith that total fairness towards Roman Catholicism can be productive not only of peace, which is essential, but for a material measure of support of the British connection'.

This was always unlikely, and indeed many Catholics resented O'Neill's attempts to seduce them with such weak inducements as 'civic weeks' (community festivals). The People's Democracy, a radical civil rights organization, in early 1969 angrily denounced his 'false picture of a happily integrated community rollicking in a prosperous Unionist paradise' as a 'gimmick designed to entice the entire community into the Unionist fold'. Most Catholics were rather less negative, but even the moderate Roman Catholic Cardinal Conway disparaged O'Neillism in an interview in March 1969: 'I think many Unionists underestimate the capacity of people to see when they are being fobbed off with words and gestures. Our people are not at all impressed, for example, when civic weeks and visits to Catholic schools seemed to be chalked up as much needed reform.' Indeed, the continuation of discriminatory practices served to render O'Neill's soft rhetoric hollow in many Catholics' ears.

Throughout 1967 and 1968 a propaganda war was waged. Unionists spoke of a coming new era of community reconciliation, and Catholic activists contrasted this rhetoric to the continued persistence of discriminatory practices. The Northern Ireland Civil Rights Association (NICRA) drew explicitly on the model of civil rights agitation developed by blacks in the United States of America. This was an innovation, in that it was explicitly non-political. Rather than tie up allegations of anti-Catholic discrimination with traditional nationalist objections to the border, the new wave of agitation asked merely for 'British rights for British citizens'. In fact, this was primarily a tactic to embarrass the Unionist government before British and international public opinion. Few Catholics were genuinely willing to forgo their nationalist aspirations. Few Catholics had any intention of tearing down partition immediately, nor did they believe this to be possible. For many, impressed by the liberalism and shared prosperity of the United Kingdom, some form of common citizenship with Britain was to be welcomed. Their demands for an end to discrimination within the Northern Ireland state, pure and simple, was genuine enough. But equally they were keen to delegitimize Stormont rule and content if disorder in the province reminded the world that they were primarily Irish, not contented subjects of the crown. They had no intention of trading civil rights for national aspirations.

The civil rights movement

Though good propaganda, activists still had difficulty in attracting much attention from outside Northern Ireland. This changed on 5 October 1968 when a civil rights march in Derry, manipulated by radicals intent on a confrontation, was violently dispersed by Royal Ulster Constabulary (RUC) officers wielding batons. Television cameras captured dramatic images of police brutality and the insurrectionary riots that briefly flared in the Catholic Bogside during the following two nights. In the 'fifty-day revolution' that followed, civil rights demonstrations spread across the north.

Attempts to break them by police repression failed due to the relative weakness of police resources available to the Stormont government. The Special Powers Act contained a battery of fearsome powers, from internment to flogging, but was embarrassingly draconian. In times of emergency the auxiliary (and wholly Protestant) B-Specials could be called upon, and indeed they had historically been given quite some latitude. One B-Special, later a loyalist paramilitary member, recalled: 'In our area we did more or less as we liked . . . knew all the Roman Catholics and kept close watch on them. Sometimes some of the lads gave them a roughing up—I'm not saying that went on a lot but the politicians never complained then.' But while these resources were effective in counter-insurgency, they lacked the subtlety to deal with a delicate public-order situation. Professional and impartial policing was called for. By the end of November 1968 RUC numbers stood at 3,168. However, while police forces in Britain could draw reinforcements from adjacent districts, this was not an option available in the province. Thus for an anti-Vietnam War demonstration on 27 November in London's Grosvenor Square, 8,000 police managed 15–20,000 marchers. For a 16 November civil rights demonstration in Derry, with a similar number on the streets, the normal RUC presence of 130 could only be raised to 400.

Lacking the ability to smother protests by weight of numbers, march prohibitions could only be enforced with extreme state aggression. But with television cameras present to relay police infractions back to an unsympathetic British audience, this was not really an option. Before another technically illegal march, Detective Inspector Ross McGimpsey sent out a message: 'I wish Non Commissioned Officers to impress on all men under their command that a very critical audience of press, radio and television persons will have their sights focused on them and that the dignity, firmness and tact of our police force must be clearly evident.'

The only alternative was concession, yet Unionists were loathe to give way before street politics and, indeed, the dictates of Harold Wilson's Labour government at Westminster. On 4 November Wilson summoned Terence O'Neill and his cabinet colleagues to Downing Street to demand reforms. These finally were delivered on 27 November. O'Neill put forward a five-point plan: fairer allocation of housing, an impartial ombudsman to investigate complaints against the government, an end to company votes in council elections, a review of the Special Powers Act, and a Londonderry

Development Corporation to displace the gerrymandered council. 'One man one vote', the catch-cry of the civil rights movement, was not mentioned.

Catholics were not satisfied with these reforms. They were inadequate in themselves and, perhaps more worrying still, they threatened to return the propaganda advantage to the Unionists. Nevertheless, as demonstrations continued and attracted loyalist counter-demonstrations, organized principally by the Protestant cleric and political hard-liner Ian Paisley, much middle-of-the-road opinion feared a complete breakdown of public order. Terence O'Neill capitalized on this in an emotive television broadcast early in December, when he called for time to allow reforms to be implemented: 'Your voice has been heard and clearly heard. Your duty now is to play your part in taking the heat out of the situation before blood is shed.' Catholics were even more impressed when O'Neill accepted the resignation of his intractable minister of home affairs, William Craig.

Violence develops

The truce was soon broken, however, when radicals set off on a 'long march' from Belfast to Derry on 1 January 1969. Their deliberate intention was to deprive the government of time to stabilize its position. Having travelled through many unwelcoming Protestant areas, they were savagely attacked by a loyalist mob at Burntollet Bridge on 4 January. It was lucky that none died. Amongst those attacking were off-duty members of the police auxiliary, the B-Specials. As the marchers straggled into Derry, rioting reignited in the Catholic areas. A later government report found that a 'number of policemen were guilty of misconduct which involved assault and battery, malicious damage to property . . . and the use of provocative sectarian and political slogans'. The RUC had to be withdrawn, creating for the first time (if briefly) a 'no go' area effectively outside the direct control of the state.

The following week a badly organized civil rights march in Newry dissolved into violence, and, fearful of losing their martyr status, even the radicals agreed to a cessation of demonstrations for a period. However, the failure of O'Neill to secure order despite his concession of reforms provoked massive disunity within the hitherto monolithic Unionist Party. To quell dissent, he called a general election for 24 February, but though he succeeded in securing a bare majority of support in the new parliament, he signally failed to attract Catholic voters. The O'Neillite project, of winning sections of the minority around to a rebranded unionism, had failed.

O'Neill's attempt to shift the rhetoric of unionism, and some mild attempts to ameliorate discrimination against Catholics, riled a section of ultra-Protestant opinion. Working-class and rural Protestants in particular stuck rigidly to their conception of the state as exclusive property of the Protestant people. From the mid-1960s the growing alienation of grassroots loyalists seriously perturbed mainstream unionism. Could reforms and rhetoric really win over Catholics, or was O'Neill running the risk of fragmenting the unionist alliance? Might not the unionist monolith be weakened to the extent that an anti-unionist alliance would be capable of wresting power from the custodians of the constitution?

Conclusion

The Stormont regime was unquestionably democratic and, in its welfare policies and subsidation of Catholic education, rather liberal by the standards of the day. Discrimination was limited in scale, but pervasive and consistent, designed to preserve two communal blocks in which Protestant Unionism was to retain an unwavering majority. The symbolic apparatus of the state—its sponsored festivals, holidays, statues, etc—was exclusively Unionist. Ulster's quasi-official national day was the explicitly anti-Roman Catholic Orange 12 July. Catholics sulked, or when they fought it was not only to reform the state, but to discredit it, to humiliate it as they had been humiliated. This was the liberating spirit for Catholics of the civil rights movement. Terence O'Neill believed that Catholics could, if treated fairly, be won over to a reformed unionism. The majority of Unionists did not share this optimism, however, and preferred the solidity of communal politics. They read the civil rights movement as anti-state, rather than a campaign for admission to the full rights of citizens. Their reaction increasingly was to treat the movement as an embryonic nationalist insurgency.

3

Life Cheapens: The Descent into War

The strategy of tension

As early as 1966 a shadowy paramilitary group, the Ulster Volunteer Force (named after the 1912 UVF), with some connections to the extremes of mainstream unionism, attempted to scupper O'Neillism by imitating republican violence. The UVF hoped to entrench existing polarities between communities and destroy illusions that Catholics could be loyal to the state. This coolly rational plan collapsed due to the sectarian enthusiasm of its members. In May it targeted a Catholic pub, mistakenly killing a Protestant woman; when in June it assassinated a Catholic man, Terence O'Neill declared the UVF illegal.

Loyalist political violence quickly regained renewed effect with the civil rights movement. Unionists in 1968 found themselves confronted by a movement that threatened to massively delegitimize their regime in British and indeed international public opinion. The spontaneous reaction of many loyalists was to provoke a sectarian clarification. A suitably hard-line unionist response would rally Protestant forces and by aggressively identifying any opposition with nationalist subversion, generate a self-fulfilling prophecy. Repression would provoke atavistic republicanism, which unionists felt sure lay behind civil rights rhetoric. Deluded British and liberal fellow-travellers would see Catholic aspirations in their true light. Action could then be taken to suppress the republican hardcore. To this end there was a concerted conspiratorial campaign from the unionist right to induce sectarian confrontation.

At first Stormont itself, its law and order policies directed by the firebrand Minister of Home Affairs, Bill Craig, seemed up to the task of physically and politically ghettoizing civil rights protesters. The march of 5 October 1968 in Derry was rerouted to peg it into the Catholic and nationalist Bogside. Attempts by the RUC to enforce this violently, however, sparked serious rioting. From this point the state was forced to tread carefully in arbitrarily limiting the right to free demonstration. For loyalists, Catholic nationalists were being given a free run at depicting themselves falsely as citizens simply claiming rights.

Counter-demonstrations

Ian Paisley, with his sidekick Major Roy Bunting command-ing the Protestant Volunteer Force, was determined to expose the marchers. His strategy was to block civil rights demonstrations at sectarian interfaces, thus outing them as foreign nationalist intrusions into unionist territory. As an added advantage, the police would be compelled to enforce this ghettoization to prevent major breaches of the peace. As early as October 1968 a student march was blocked on the way to Belfast city centre, at the intersection of the university district and the loyalist Sandy Row.

The most serious such provocation was the wholesale occupation of Armagh city by loyalists to prevent a civil rights gathering on 30 November 1968. At this point the RUC began to fear a civil war. When loyalists harried a civil rights 'long march' from Belfast to Derry in early January 1969, eventually attacking it at Burntollet Bridge on its final day, the strategy of tension threatened to overreach itself. The following Saturday a civil rights demonstration in Newry degenerated into rioting, to the embarrassment of the organizers, who had been enjoying the moral high ground. This marked the end of a phase for both sides. Civil rights marches were suspended until late February, and never regained their centrality. The loyalists, meanwhile, switched tactics.

Loyalist violence

The change was dramatically announced by a concerted loyalist bombing campaign deliberately aping IRA tactics. In March and April 1969 loyalists set off a series of explosions in the hope that they would be blamed on the IRA. On 20 April an attack on the Silent Valley reservoir in the Mourne mountains cut off Belfast's water supply. This was in the context of widespread rioting in Catholic areas after the election of

Bernadette Devlin (a civil rights radical enjoying tacit republican support) to Mid-Ulster in a by-election on 18 April. To many unionists, O'Neill appeared to be presiding over an incipient nationalist revolt, and he was forced from office on 28 April. O'Neill himself claimed that he had been 'literally blown from office'. He was replaced by James Chichester-Clarke. It did not end here, however.

Loyalist aggression against Catholic areas continued in the months following. 'Pub rioting', concentrated on the Belfast Edenderry Inn, a north Belfast flashpoint, became ominously regular from May 1969. The Shankill Defence Force, commanded by John McKeague, indicated direction behind what at first appeared to be casual violence. On 14 June they joined the RUC in blocking a republican demonstration from the centre of Belfast. Aggression centred on Catholic strongholds abutting or enclosed in Protestant areas in Belfast, notably Unity Flats. On 2 August a crowd of 200 descended from the Shankill to smash all the windows in these flats. At the interfaces, Catholic families began to move to safer areas.

The loyalist attempt to clarify the battle lines was working as expected. Nationalism in the Catholic community had never been repudiated and, as the forces of Unionist aggression moved into battle array, the military traditions of the republican movement acquired renewed relevance. IRA recruitment posters appeared in Dundalk, republican marches superseded civil rights excursions, and the hardmen were anxiously turned to in Catholic areas as those best qualified to organize defence. This in turn screwed up tension, as Protestants perceived the reorganization of militant republicanism and readied themselves for the challenge of an insurrection. The situation exploded in August 1969.

August '69

Protracted rioting throughout the province in July and August had already stretched the RUC to the limit when an Apprentice Boys parade in Londonderry on 12 August sparked a three-day siege of the Catholic Bogside. Catholics battled to keep out the RUC and B-Specials, which they now dismissed as little more than sectarian forces in uniform. The RUC were blocked by Rossville high-rise flats, from the top of which they were showered by petrol bombs. This was all part of a prepared defence: the nationalist Bogside, Brandywell, and Creggan areas were ringed with 42 barricades. From midnight on 12 August the RUC employed CS (or tear) gas. In the following two days 1,091 cartridges and 161 grenades of gas pummelled the Bogside. There was something curiously choreographed about the affair, and indeed as an exotic street theatre it was lapped up by the world's press and television.

As mutual exhaustion set in, however, the entirely Protestant paramilitary police—the B-Specials—were moved into Waterloo Place in readiness to join the assault. They were never deployed. On the afternoon of 14 August, head of the RUC Inspector General Joseph Anthony Peacock asked for the British army to be deployed and around 5 p.m. the first soldiers of the Prince of Wales regiment arrived on the streets of Derry.

Spreading demonstrations in solidarity with the Bogside developed into aggressive Catholic rioting in Belfast. The RUC, and certainly Protestant mobs, assumed that some form of nationlist insurrection was underway. This activated the Protestant desire for pre-emptive action, and a generalized assault on Catholic areas in Belfast was launched in an attempt to destroy the territorial base of internal subversion. A government report recorded that:

> On the night of the 14th, the worst violence of the 1969 disturbances occurred in Belfast, notably in the Ardoyne and on the Falls Road. The police, who believed by now that they were facing an armed uprising, used guns, including Browning machine-guns mounted on Shorland armoured vehicles. Four Catholics were shot dead by police fire: one Protestant was killed by a shot fired by a rioter in Divis Street. Catholic houses were burnt by Protestants, especially in the Conway Street area. The only clear evidence of direct IRA participation in these riots occurred at the St. Comgall's School in Divis Street, where automatic fire was directed against the police. On the same night there was a riot in Armagh, as a result of which a Catholic man was killed by USC fire.
>
> By the morning of 15 August the police were exhausted. They failed to control the violence which broke out that day on the Crumlin Road and in the Clonard area of the city. Nor did they prevent the burning of factories by Catholics and public houses by Protestants. It has to be admitted that the police were no longer in control of the city. On the evening of

the 15th, the [British] Army entered the Falls Road, but not the Crumlin Road, which was the scene of a serious confrontation between Protestants and Catholics. Two people—one Protestant and one Catholic—died by civilian shooting in Belfast on 15 August. Catholic houses were burnt that night by Protestants at Bombay Street (Falls Road area) and Brookfield Street (Crumlin Road). On the evening of 16 August, the Army entered the Crumlin Road and thereafter the disturbances died away.

Though it generally commended police restraint, the report admitted six serious breakdowns of discipline. This conduct, the author averred, 'was due very largely to the belief held at the time by many of the police, including senior officers, that they were dealing with an armed uprising engineered by the IRA'.

Clearly the RUC had been effectively pulled along by the strategy of tension. Their employment of armoured cars and heavy machine-guns against what they thought was republican rebellion was wildly inappropriate in the actual circumstances of communal turmoil. In the aftermath loyalists spoke wistfully of '48 hours'; had the army taken another two days to deploy, Belfast would have been cleared entirely of Catholics. As it was the boundary between the Lower Falls and the Lower Shankill became sharply defined, quickly reinforced by the erection of walls of corrugated sheets of iron bolted to metal posts sunk in concrete, the 'peace lines'. British opinion was shocked. A young reporter, Max Hastings, saw the RUC machine-gunning Catholic homes: 'Anyone who was there that August night in Belfast . . .

understood how the revival of the IRA became possible, and why the Royal Ulster Constabulary forfeited for ever the trust of Catholic Ireland.'

The British army

With the introduction of troops as a support to the police, an army commander had taken overall charge of law and order. Politically this was backed up by close supervision from the home secretary at Westminster, and a permanent British official ensconced in the office next door to that of the Northern Ireland prime minister. Beyond this, however, the British government would not go. They feared being sucked into the Irish bog. Northern Ireland's devolved government was left in place, despite massive Catholic alienation. The British army was merely to support the civil power, in nationalist eyes to help the Protestants keep down the Catholics.

The British army, as the historical antithesis of Irish nationalism, never received more than a temporary and partial welcome from Catholic areas, even when relieving them from loyalist siege. Their presence, however, had militarized the Catholic ghettos—in an astounding abdication of responsibility the mainland police had refused to countenance serving in Northern Ireland—and the consequent military theatre invited a nationalist military response.

This was not initially clear. Indeed, Protestants were angered at the state-sponsored reforms designed to placate

6 Troops arrive in Belfast, 1969. Their honeymoon was to be short

Catholics, particularly the abolition of the B-Specials and the disarming (temporary as it proved) of the RUC. In October 1969 during serious rioting on the Shankill Road an RUC man was shot dead and thirteen soldiers were wounded by Protestant gunmen. Eventually the troops were ordered to return fire and killed two Protestants. The British army showed no partiality to Protestant rioters, and quelled them with a stern hand.

Even such a brusque check could only slow loyalist pressure. From late 1969 to mid-1970 loyalism held the initiative. Intimidation squeezed Catholic districts and a campaign of bombs and assassination threats kept the security forces keyed up and the political temperature high. Over the next few years Protestant intimidation largely succeeded in clearing disloyal elements from contested terrain. In 1974 a Community Relations Commission report said that firm evidence existed of 8,180 families having been forced to evacuate their homes in the Greater Belfast area between August 1969 and February 1973, 80 per cent of whom they estimated to be Catholic. Around 60,000 Belfast people (around 10 per cent of the population) had been forced to leave their homes. A situation was created in which disloyal populations could be contained and repressed en masse with the intention of drawing out and eliminating armed opposition to the state.

As a strategy designed to isolate and provoke Catholic nationalism, it enjoyed much success. Unionist politicians lost all credibility with the Catholic population as neutral arbiters; armed self-defence was the wholly natural response to the loyalist bombing and intimidation campaign. The IRA developed as the cutting edge of this defence. As the IRA shook itself up and began to organize, the British army, now called in to support the 'civil power', found itself moving inexorably towards war with Irish republicanism.

The Provisional IRA

Catholic politics had received a profound shock by the events of August 1969. Hundreds of nationalist homes had been burnt down. There was massive displacement of population, principally into nationalist ghettos from mixed areas in Belfast. The Dublin government established emergency refugee centres. Indeed, the southern government led by Jack Lynch, mindful of its claim of sovereignty over the north, had raised nationalist hopes and unionist fears of intervention by the Republic's army during the violence when it declared that it would not stand 'idly by'. In the months following it sponsored a paper, *Voice of the North*, to pump out anti-partition propaganda and a handful of northern nationalists were spirited across the border to receive arms training at army camps. Moves were made to provide arms for the defence of nationalist communities. All this was rapidly reversed, however, as Britain got wind. Involvement in the developing Ulster troubles could only destabilize the south. And, as Lynch gloomily informed northern nationalists seeking aid: 'If we were given a gift of Northern Ireland tomorrow, we could not accept it.' Neither economically nor politically could the Republic hope to absorb the truculent north.

Northern nationalists thus had to shift for themselves. The historic defenders of the Catholic community, at least in theory, were the IRA. But by the 1960s they had reached a low ebb. A military campaign of little effect launched in 1956, Operation Harvest, had been called off in 1962 due to the lethargy of the nationalist people. Eleven republicans and six RUC men had been killed. Under a new leadership, the movement began painfully and slowly to reorientate towards political agitation under a leftist political banner. In 1967 IRA chief of staff Cathal Goulding publicly downgraded the traditional republican reliance on 'physical force' and announced a radical socialist agenda. Poorly armed, the IRA played a minimal role in the defence of Catholic areas in August 1969, for fear of stoking up the conflagration. Northern republicans were humiliated as 'IRA—I Ran Away' graffiti appeared on riot-scarred walls.

The southern leadership, however, was more concerned to build itself up as a credible socialist movement. It aimed to drop the long-standing policy of abstention, in which no republican would sit in the 'illegal' Dublin parliament. This proved the last straw for IRA militants, many of whom had long resented the movement's drift towards Marxism. In September 1969 militants took control of the IRA in Belfast. In December they were joined by southern traditionalists, and the republican movement formally split into Official and Provisional wings. The Officials were pulled into violence in the north, though were consistently less aggressive than the

Provisionals (or Provos). In 1972 they declared a ceasefire, and in the following years repudiated insurrectionary violence. The Provos became, in effect, the inheritors of the 'physical force' republican tradition. Out of the ashes of Bombay Street, went the mantra for decades following, rose the Provisional IRA.

As the IRA organized in Catholic areas, the British army treated it almost as recognized enemy, often meeting it in order to reduce friction with the civilian population. But battering Protestants and hob-nobbing with the IRA was political anathema for the Unionist government at Stormont. With the election of the Conservative Heath government at Westminister in June 1970, the reins on Stormont appear to have been loosened. Unionists demanded that the army bring down Catholic barricades in Derry and Belfast and resume normal policing in these areas. On the other hand, the failure to ban Orange processions in July 1970 led to severe communal confrontations and a renewed Catholic fear of another 'August '69'.

Unremitting pressure on Catholic areas created anew the IRA. The British army, keen to identify a clear military target in the shape of a centrally organized subversive opponent, adopted the loyalist preference for isolation and repression of Catholic areas in an attempt to draw out and engage the IRA. This search for a military response, however, underestimated the tenacity of Irish republican ideology.

Republicanism

The IRA drew on a long and important tradition in Irish nationalism. Nineteenth-century nationalist concepts of military revolution fetishized armed conflict as the true crucible of nations—little surprise in an era of blood, iron, and imperialism. Even Redmond's moderate brand of home rule nationalism looked for vindication on the bloody battlefields of the First World War. Republicanism had long accepted democratic ideals, but as early as the Fenian constitution it determined that the essential sovereignty of Ireland as a whole was inalienable—that is, no interest group, even if that were the majority of the Irish people at any particular point in time, had the right to repudiate complete Irish independence.

Even if only a tiny minority held secure to the ideal of unfettered Irish sovereignty, the Irish Republic, 'virtually existing' in the hearts and minds of true patriots, had the right to insist upon the complete loyalty of all Irish citizens. With such authority, radical nationalists believed they were morally entitled to exact retribution, up to and including the death penalty, for all those who treacherously refused the call of the nation. An analogous notion might be that of De Gaulle's Free French: the Vichy regime was illegitimate because it bartered away what could not be sold, French sovereignty. Thus the French Resistance, though without a tested mandate for much of its struggle, felt itself morally correct in waging war against the regime and exacting retribution on all collaborators.

The constitution of the Irish Republican Brotherhood, passed in 1867, declared, 'the Supreme Council of the IRB is hereby declared in fact, as well as by right, the sole Government of the Irish Republic. Its enactments shall be the laws of the Irish Republic until Ireland secures absolute national independence, and a permanent Republican Government is established.'

If this ethos motivated hard-line nationalists in the nineteenth century, it had relatively little practical effect as long as revolution was perceived in terms of mass insurrection and conventional warfare. Until the forces of the virtual republic took to the field, sanctions against the uncommitted majority were unlikely to be undertaken. They were, to a degree, in the 1916 Rising. The proclamation issued by the rebels announced 'the right of the people of Ireland to the ownership of Ireland, and to the unfettered control of Irish destinies, to be sovereign and indefeasible. The long usurpation of that right by a foreign people and government has not extinguished the right, nor can it ever be extinguished except by the destruction of the Irish people. . . . The Irish republic is entitled to, and hereby claims, the allegiance of every Irishman and Irishwoman.'

It took the evolution of a new form of warfare from 1919 in Ireland to generate new coercive powers on behalf of the virtual republic. Sinn Féin's dramatic victory in the 1918 general election, winning 73 out of 105 seats, for the first time indicated a democratic mandate for independence, at least for Catholic Ireland. The initial republican strategy had been to win recognition for Irish independence by creating facts on the ground—a separatist parliamentary assembly (the Dáil), local government pledging allegiance to the Dáil, a judicial system separate from the crown, and military formations to replace those of the British state. A new insurrection and war was not expected when Sinn Féin went to the country with their strategy of withdrawing from the United Kingdom political system in 1919.

The failure of the new para-state to gain recognition either from Britain or the international community left the Irish National Volunteers in an invidious position. Were they, self-declared army of the Republic, to stand aside while the crown defied and repressed the Dáil government? The Dáil itself avoided the issue, but a vanguard of IRA ideologues and hard-men increasingly took offensive action against crown forces. A heavy-handed British response muffled popular disquiet at IRA actions, and by 1920 the war had quickly escalated.

This was a war of a particular kind, however. Whilst guerrilla conflict was not new, it had hitherto served as an adjunct to conventional warfare. Hopelessly outclassed in armaments, training, and numbers, the IRA could not hope to contest with crown forces directly in the field. Initial tactics—seizing arms, defying arrest, selective assassinations, undermining the British administration—developed into a strategy of guerrilla warfare in which irregular soldiers relied upon popular sympathy to provide cover while they harried their opponents. The British government, not unnaturally, refused to accept this as legitimate armed action, and condemned the IRA as worse than rebels. In Lloyd George's parlance, the IRA were simply 'murder gangs'.

The IRA itself was bothered by its irregular status—revolutionary people's war being an uncomfortable novelty—and in so far as was possible, aped conventional military structures, complete with battalions, companies, officer ranks, etc., all borrowed from British army manuals. Activists dreamed of somehow converting their strategy into something approaching conventional war and concocted hopeless schemes for creating liberated zones from which they could operate en masse. Despite the risks and difficulty in scoring 'kills', operations against crown 'hard-targets', in the form of ambushes, were generally preferred as being more prestigious than attacks on civilian 'collaborators'. The unarmed Dublin Metropolitan Police were left alone.

Thus IRA 'terrorism' was born with a significant admixture of conventional military morality. Soldiers of the Republic hoped to validate their shadow state by replicating in miniature norms of soldiering. Indeed, it was large-scale confrontations (the Kilmichael ambush, the assault on Dublin Customs House) that helped create an environment in which the British government persuaded itself that it was valid to negotiate with representatives of gunmen.

Nevertheless, Britain's negotiating stance was partly motivated by a desire to strip the IRA of its legitimacy. The 1921 Anglo-Irish treaty offered substantially less than the longed-for Republic. Most gallingly southern Ireland, styled the Free State, formally remained under the crown. The bulk of the IRA, who had always put adherence to the ideal of the

Republic over loyalty to the representatives of the people, rejected the Dáil vote that, on 7 January 1922, approved the treaty by 64 votes for, 57 against. Sovereignty remained inalienable, and the IRA declared those members of the Dáil in favour of the treaty to have forfeited their right to speak for the nation. They declared their allegiance to the dwindling anti-treaty remnants of the Second Dáil, in purist eyes the only legitimate government of Ireland. The IRA's brief enjoyment of a quasi-democratic mandate was at an end.

Britain, eager to exact vengeance on the IRA irreconcilables who had humiliatingly fought them to stalemate, financed and armed an entirely new Free State army. Having 'won the war', the IRA found itself alienated from the new state. Though unwilling at first to fight a native government as it had the British, it was equally unwilling to accept the new dispensation by demobilizing. The Free State, naturally, found the existence of a powerful political army beyond its control intolerable. Kevin O'Higgins, speaking for the pro-treaty Dáil, declared: 'We will not have two governments in this country and we will not have two armies: they cannot have it both ways. They cannot have the platform and the bomb.' Acting on this, they suppressed the pretensions of the IRA in the civil war of 1922–3.*

The IRA lost the civil war, but maintained itself in existence as representative of the Republic, claiming that only the

* Dáil Éireann, Volume 5, 14 December, 1923, http://www.oireachtas-debates. gov.ie/

Dáil of 1919–21 was legitimate, as those who had accepted the treaty had illegally compromised inalienable Irish sovereignty. As De Valera led anti-treaty republicans inexorably into constitutional politics, the IRA suffered a steady decline in the south of Ireland. Its quasi-legal theology returned directly to Fenian traditions when, in 1939, the dwindling old guard of the anti-treaty Dáil members elected to discharge their power of 'government' directly to the IRA Army Council. This remained a key point of principle during the long years of IRA insurgency in the Northern Ireland Troubles. As the IRA bible, the 'Green Book', put it:

> the [Irish Republic] Army is the direct representative of the 1918 Dáil Éireann parliament, and that as such they are the legal and lawful government of the Irish Republic, which has the moral right to pass laws for, and to claim jurisdiction over . . . all of its people regardless of creed or loyalty

The IRA's status as victors in the war of independence, a glorious heritage the southern Irish state found hard to match, allowed it to persist as a feature of national life. If political paramilitarism, hardly uncommon in the inter-war period, was discredited in Europe by Communism and Nazism, Ireland and the IRA remained shielded from this catastrophic experience. As late as 1966 it was accorded quasi-official status when it provided a guard of honour for the returning remains of Roger Casement, a leader of the 1916 Rising executed in Britain. In the 1921 treaty, Britain had hoped to divide republicans and eradicate the radicals. In doing so they unwittingly created a powerful tradition of revanchist paramilitarism that was to explode in their faces in 1971.

The IRA, in common with Irish nationalists generally, never accepted the legitimacy of partition. Though they recognized that Ulster Unionists were opposed to an independent united Ireland, they believed that this opposition was based not on the slow gestation of national sentiment, but the religious bigotry, British-fostered privileges, and false fears of Protestants. Partition mutilated a true nation in the interests of an ephemeral elite. They were fond of quoting Abraham Lincoln on the attempted partition of the United States during the American Civil War: 'On what rightful principle may a state, being not more than one-fifth part of the Nation in soil and population, break up the Nation and then cause a proportionately large sub-division of itself in a most arbitrary way?' (It is ironic that many Irish nationalists in the 1860s had identified with the southern states as fellow fighters for secession.) As the southern states, once coerced, accepted and benefited from their membership of the American nation, so too, Irish nationalists fondly believed, would Ulster Protestants. Curiously, this was much the same logic Britain had applied to Irish nationalists in the nineteenth century.

Though republicanism was, ideologically, non-sectarian and democratic, it would be idle to deny the religious passions that often underlay it. Volunteers were usually observant Catholics, and this could leak into the imagery of their struggle (prisoners churned out hand-crafted crosses to adorn the homes of sympathizers). As a representative of the Irish government in the 1950s, Conor Cruise O'Brien met with rural nationalists: 'For the sake of breaking the silence, I asked: "How many Protestants are there around here?" He replied, slowly and deliberately: "In this townland [rural district], we have only one Protestant. . . . And with the help of God . . . we'll have him out of it by Christmas."' It remained bad manners to voice such sentiments, but the mask could slip. Eamonn McCann in the 1990s attended a republican meeting in Derry to hear the speaker rage against 'unionists, Orange Tories, Protestants, call them what you will'. Hostility to neighbours was sublimated into hatred for 'the Brits'. The irony was, however, that in the final analysis republicans depended upon Britain to 'persuade' or coerce Protestants into a united Ireland.

Provo psychology

The IRA appeared to be coming to the end of its shelf-life when it was rejuvenated by the Northern Irish Troubles. It drew upon a ready store of mythology and practice—the indefeasible republic, militarism, and (in the north) defenders of the Catholic community—when confronted by loyalist pressure and the presence of the British army. In mid-1970 it quickly displaced the loyalists as the prime perpetrator of bombing and in 1971 turned to attacks on its perceived counterpart, the British army.

The evident militarization of society from the arrival of the British army on the streets in August 1969 called for an 'Irish' response. The IRA garnered legitimacy as the army of the 'people', representing the martial prowess of the Irish nation for a substantial section of the Ulster Catholic community. The armed struggle itself was a source of national pride for the republican constituency, a militant refusal to be assimilated or subordinated. In this respect, the movement was more important than the final aim. Indeed, Catholics broadly speaking were prepared to countenance a political settlement well short of a united, independent Ireland, as was indicated by continuing support for the moderate Social Democratic and Labour Party (SDLP). Moreover Catholics were confident that inexorable processes of demographic movement and the diminishing of borders in an integrated Europe would lead to communal Catholic victory. The relative moderation of Catholic political demands appears at odds with the widespread support for armed struggle. But in time of conflict, many wanted their own Irish army.

If IRA actions are looked upon as symbolic rather than functional, this, and the longevity of the campaign, may be better understood. Recalled one volunteer (their term for members), Hugh McMonagle:

> I remember running down and seeing the soldiers had sealed off William Street. I remember being fascinated by all these soldiers with their helmets and rifles and backpacks. I was totally amazed at them and excited by them. I said, 'I am going to be a soldier someday.'
>
> [*Interviewer*] Did you join the army?
> [*McMonagle*] I didn't join that particular army, no. I ended up joining the opposition.

The British army was well aware of the developing IRA, but, given the collapse of normal policing in the Catholic ghettos, lacked hard intelligence. They reckoned the IRA was a ramshackle outfit. A 1972 intelligence report recorded perhaps prejudiced impressions:

> It showed that the Provisional gunmen were usually unemployed, working-class Catholics, some of whom would probably have been ordinary criminals if it were not for the movement. . . . They were mostly young, under 23, and those who survived did so because they were 'street-wise' and cunning. . . . The greatest single factor in their joining the Provisional IRA was a family connection. . . . Surprisingly little time, if any, would be spent in the serious discussion of IRA business or operations. . . . They bothered little with their weapons, and the average gunman was unable to strip down the weapon he used, or even deal with a jam.

In light of this, security forces elected to grip the Catholic ghettos by the scruff of the neck; a good shaking would raise a dust cloud of low-level intelligence sufficient to illuminate the decentralized and *ad hoc* structure of their opponents. High-profile and intrusive 'foot patrols' would incessantly stop and question the population, carry out vehicle checks, and search houses to hoover up a mass of 'contact-information'. From this would be built a detailed and comprehensive profile of their area of operations and its inhabitants in an attempt to uncover the Provisional IRA's organization, membership, and activities. In 1971 there were 17,000 house searches, usually none too gentle, rising to 36,000 in 1972 and 75,000 in 1973 and 1974. Between 1971 and 1976 there were some 250,000 house searches. Between 1 April 1973 and 1 April 1974 no less than four million vehicles were stopped and searched. Catholic civilians, unsurprisingly, saw this as the actions of an occupation army.

Republican violence escalated as the moral barriers to political violence eroded. At first the republicans stood on the defensive, organizing community defence and often negotiating with army authorities. Recruitment, arms training, and vigilante duty hardened communities to the idea of military activity. Loyalists maintained a low level of bombing and assassination threat throughout 1970. This eased the slow emergence of IRA aggression, its own bombing missions intended, as much as anything, to allow volunteers to blow off steam. The shame of August 1969 was symbolically erased in June 1970 when a Provo sniper nest in the grounds of St Matthew's Roman Catholic Church held off a loyalist assault on the Catholic Short Strand. The British army refused to move, instead sealing off bridges to isolate east Belfast from the city centre. Six thousand Catholics were surrounded by 60,000 Protestants. For many Catholics, the IRA were re-vindicated as the authentic community defenders.

Militarism

The emergence of a structured subversive organization, drawing support from the minority community, made a much more appealing target for the British army than inchoate loyalism. It responded with enthusiasm to the challenge presented by such a clear-cut and identifiable target. The solution was militaristic. A definitive end to the British army's reliance on winning Catholic 'hearts and minds' was marked by the Ballymurphy riots in west Belfast at the beginning of April 1970. The army believed these to have been deliberately engineered by the IRA, and responded with warlike ferocity. In a remarkable escalation, the British army stated that petrol bombers, by now primarily Catholic, were 'liable to be shot'. The Provisional IRA retaliated, threatening to shoot soldiers. By late 1970 it would appear that the British government adopted a 'lance the boil' policy, i.e. escalating the level of violence to the point where the IRA would overstretch and expose itself to definitive counter-blows.

Catholic areas were treated as IRA strongholds, to be saturated and provoked in the hope of drawing out the gunmen, who in turn could be eliminated. For 35 hours between 3 and 5 July 1970, the army imposed a curfew on some 50 streets in the Lower Falls in Belfast. Some 5,000 homes were searched for arms, and, as the IRA resisted the disarming of the area, five civilians were killed.

Paddy Devlin, a local politician, recalled:

> The army clearly believed that there were many arms hidden there and that after the violence of the previous weeks (mainly by the provisionals) a deliberate confrontation with these challengers was called for. As violent clashes developed and intensified throughout the evening CS gas canisters were lobbed into the area by the military. A helicopter, with an underslung loudspeaker, descended to virtual roof level and a

voice announced that the area was under curfew and anyone on the streets after the warning would be shot. . . . Shooting increased in tempo as darkness fell. The high pitched whine of the armoured cars as they manoeuvred round the narrow streets filled me with dread. The shooting only stopped at dawn. . . . Daylight brought the follow up search by the military. They axed doors down that could easily have been opened, ripped up floorboards, broke furniture unnecessarily and tipped the contents of drawers and cupboards all over the place.

Soldiers were reported to take particular pleasure in destroying Catholic religious imagery during house raids.

Even at this point the IRA was unwilling to escalate into a war. As Danny Morrison, a leader in Sinn Féin, explained, 'There was no way at that time that the IRA could have shot Brits or policemen. . . . They couldn't have sold it [to the people]. The reaction of people would have been "God Almighty, did we produce people who are capable of doing that?"' Britain, however, was rather more keen. As early as June 1971 Reginald Maudling, the Conservative British home secretary, announced that the British government was now 'at war with the IRA'.

Perceived by many as community defenders, the IRA was free to enforce an increasingly brutal martial law, in accordance with its self-percieved status as the government of the 'republic'. Criminals and those who 'fraternized with the enemy' were punished, often by tarring and feathering. This served further to cut off Catholic areas from formal state authority, and to isolate British military forces within these

The human cost, 2001

More than 3,600 people have died, approximately 90 per cent at the hands of illegal paramilitaries. Up to 1998, the IRA killed more than 1,800, just over half the total. Various republican factions killed another 231. The IRA's victims included 465 British army soldiers, 190 members of the locally recruited Ulster Defence Regiment/Royal Irish Rangers, and 272 members of the RUC. They expressly targeted 133 Protestant civilians, 91 of them in the years 1974–6. The Irish National Liberation Army added another 21.

Loyalists killed 990, of whom 708 were expressly targeted as Catholic civilians.

Since 1972, over 17,000 people have been charged with terrorist offences.

Government forces have killed 363. The British army killed 297, the Ulster Defence Regiment/Royal Irish Regiment killed 8, the RUC killed 55. Of the victims, some 145 were members of republican paramilitaries, 14 were in loyalist paramilitaries, and 192 were civilians.

Over 1,500 of all victims were in Belfast, nearly 500 in County Armagh, 'bandit country'. More than 600 deaths, one in five, were concentrated in North Belfast, a sectarian interface only a few miles square in area.

In addition, over 40,000 people have been injured, almost 3 per cent of the population. If one extrapolates these figures to Britain, some 111,000 people would have died, with 1.4 million people injured, equivalent to just under half of British deaths during the Second World War. By 1998, about one in seven of the adult population, disproportionately Catholic, had been the victim of a violent incident.

The Good Friday Agreement asserted that 'it is essential to acknowledge and address the suffering of the victims of violence as a necessary element of reconciliation'. Sadly, however, the agony of the bereaved is a burden difficult to share. Rita Restorick, mother of Stephen, the last soldier to be killed by the IRA in Northern Ireland, in 1997, recalled hearing the news of his death: 'That week is something of a haze. I remember going into the centre of Peterborough and seeing all the people rushing about their daily lives: I just wanted to stand there and scream, to tell them to stop and listen to what had happened to my son. Did they not know or care? I could not cope with all the people rushing around. I was in a daze.'

ghettos. Alleged spies and informers were executed. Partly as policy, partly as a consequence of a necessarily laborious technical learning curve, the IRA bombing campaign escalated at a pace sufficient to push on but not outstrip mass republican opinion. Bombs increased in sophistication, but remained primarily directly against commercial targets.

From 1971 the IRA launched an offensive. Using the cover of a riot, they shot down Gunner Robert Curtis, the first soldier to be killed by republican violence. Such attacks continued and increased in frequency. A month later three off-duty Scottish soldiers, two of them brothers aged 17 and 18, were lured from a Belfast pub and shot dead by the Provisionals. This was the work of a rogue unit determined to escalate the war. A wave of public revulsion, and subsequent disavowal of the action by the Provo leadership, indicated that political violence still laboured under limits of acceptability. A week later, James Chichester-Clark, the Unionist prime minister, resigned, complaining that Britain was not providing enough troops to maintain order. He was replaced by Brian Faulkner, a politician with a steely reputation. Faulkner whipped on the army, itself eager to search out and destroy a military target. As was often to be the case, security-force overreaction clouded memories of past republican atrocities and inadvertently helped legitimize the IRA as an army.

Internment

On 9 August 1971 internment—imprisonment of suspects without trial—was introduced. In a series of raids across Northern Ireland, 342 people were arrested and taken to makeshift camps. Only republicans were targeted. There was an immediate upsurge of violence and 17 people were killed during the next 48 hours. Of these 10 were Catholic civilians who were shot dead by the British army. Some 7,000 people, mainly Catholics, fled their homes in the upsurge of violence. On 16 August Joe Cahill, then chief of staff of the Provisional IRA, held a dramatic press conference to claim that only 30 IRA men had been interned. Whereas in the four months before internment was introduced, four soldiers, no policemen, and four civilians had been killed in Northern Ireland, in the four months after 30 soldiers,

11 police and UDR members, and 73 civilians were killed. The conflict escalated to new levels with Catholic working-class areas in Belfast and Derry, surrounded by barricades and openly patrolled by IRA volunteers—the so-called no-go areas—virtually seceding from Stormont rule.

Many internees were brutalized. Fourteen in the first round-up were subjected to psychological torture (hooding, exposure to 'white noise', deprivation of food and drink,

7 IRA man (Joe McCann), silhouetted against a burning barricade, the Markets, Belfast. Though not posed, this was how the IRA were keen to present themselves, as heroic defenders. McCann later died at the hands of British soldiers in suspicious circumstances

deprivation of sleep, and enforced standing against a wall). Internment added to the sense of the IRA as an army. In Long Kesh (an American air force base during the Second World War) all prisoners lived in 'cages', compounds of four Nissen huts surrounded by barbed wire. Each of three of the huts (120 ft × 24 ft) would house 40 men, with the fourth reserved for use as a canteen. Guards recognized IRA 'officers' and all communication went through the prisoners' 'officer commanding'. Prisoners were allowed to wear their own clothes. Because they could freely associate at all times, the men interned organized themselves militarily. Lectures on tactics and arms were held, and there was even drilling with dummy wooden guns. In 1973, William Whitelaw, the secretary of state, conceded this regime to convicted paramilitary prisoners as well as internees.

Internment was to continue until 5 December 1975. During that time 1,981 people were detained; 1,874 were Catholic/Republican, while 107 were Protestant/Loyalist. Sean MacStiofain, first chief of staff of the Provos, recalled that 'the result of the internment round-up and the interrogation excesses was that the British succeeded in bringing into combat not a diminished, but a vastly reinforced Republican guerrilla army'.

Bloody Sunday, on 31 January 1971, was the debacle that led to the almost complete collapse of Catholic opposition to political violence. Confronting a relatively small-scale riot the elite parachute regiment shot dead thirteen unarmed demonstrators (a fourteenth died later of wounds). One British army officer indicated perfectly the self-defeating militarism of counter-insurgency: 'When we moved on the streets we moved as if we in fact were moving against a well-armed well-trained army.' Not one of the facalities on Bloody Sunday was an IRA man. Had the British army fired on a similar crowd a month later, again targeting men of military age, they would hardly have been able to avoid enemy kills. Bloody Sunday led to a mass influx into the ranks of the Derry IRA. The relentless bombing campaign was accelerated; of the city's 150 shops only 20 were left trading. Almost one third of the 320 killed in Derry during the Troubles died in street clashes and gun battles during this period (54 of them members of the security forces).

Unwilling to fight on two fronts, the British army was concentrating on extirpating the IRA, the overt command structure of which made it apparently more vulnerable to direct strikes than the rather nebulous loyalist mobilizations. Also, no small point, the Catholics were the subversives and the minority; they were a more enticing target than the majority Protestants, loyal to the crown. Catholics increasingly believed that security forces were part of a general siege on their community. The moral authority of state forces, based upon notions of the even-handed application of law, disintegrated.

A not untypical incident in the strongly Protestant town of Portadown in July 1972 is illustrative. The annual Orange march to Drumcree Church had always passed through 'the tunnel' marking the entrance to Obins Street, a Catholic enclave. In the communal tension of 1972, this was certain to spark serious disorder. To ensure safe passage for the

Orangemen, army bulldozers cleared away Catholic barriers and fired CS gas to disperse nationalist rioters. The Orange parade was headed by a group of at least 50 men of the Ulster Defence Association (UDA), a loyalist paramilitary, who stood on either side of the road up to the tunnel. They threatened to invade the Catholic area, with the 3,000 men they held in reserve, if a shot was fired. Later that month Obins Street came under armed attack from loyalists. IRA members fired back, only to attract a security-force sweep to 'clear out IRA nests'. In the absence of a complete ban on Orange marches and with the UDA a legal vigilante organization, the security forces were in a genuine bind. But the Catholic reaction can be imagined.

Certainly sentiments of revenge loomed large in the motivations of IRA volunteers. One 'jocular' song was entitled 'My Little Armalite' (the standard IRA rifle, smuggled from the United States):

> I was stopped by a soldier, said he you are a swine,
> He beat me with his baton and he kicked me in the groin.
> I bowed and scraped, sure my manners were polite,
> Ah, but all the time I was thinking of my little Armalite.

There was a bravura too, a certain intoxication with violence. One account, by Maria Maguire, briefly a Provo member, captured well this enthusiasm for outlawry as a caper:

> On 27 January [1972] came the most prolonged incident of all, involving Meehann and seven other Volunteers and a detachment of the Scots Dragoon Guards. There was a four-hour gun-battle over the border near Forkhill, County

8 A Provo 'Loose talk costs lives' poster. In the 1970s, by consciously aping conventional wartime public information posters, the IRA hoped to bolster their military credentials

Armagh, the British acknowledging afterwards that they had fired 4,500 rounds at the Provisionals' position, although no one was hit on either side; the day's one casualty was a farmer's prize pig. Meehan strolled nonchalantly into Dundalk afterwards, and when a reporter asked him how he got on, said happily: 'we pasted them.'

In the heavily militarized urban areas, a virtual war psychosis existed. Reporters found that the civilian population understood quite sophisticated military terminology. Shoot-outs were often dramatic, prolonged affairs, far from the grubby *modus operandi* of back-street assassination. A republican remembers such a firefight in Ballymurphy estate, Belfast, in July 1972:

> We fired thousands of rounds at them. We tried to hit them from the house in Whiterock, from Corrigan Park, from Westrock and from Springhill. Bryson brought the Lewis gun up to the verandah of the flat above Mary's Shop in Springhill Avenue. He stood up on two bins with the Lewis mounted on a piece of wood held by pigeon-holes in the brickwood, and raked Corry's [a factory from which 'enemy' snipers were operating]; but they were still there.

Important was a widespread sense of martial pride. After August 1969 Irish Catholics could hardly identify with locally recruited Protestant security forces. British squaddies with Glasgow, scouse, or brummie accents were alien, and they were closely connected with deeply internalized mythologies of foreign oppression. 'Cromwell's men are here again', as a popular republican song put it. The IRA, for many in the

Catholic ghettos, provided validation for their sense of martial pride. To fight was good enough in the hothouse of early 1970s Northern Ireland. It was with this sentiment that one anti-internment song recalled the violence that greeted the introduction of internment in 1971:

On that black day in August, when Faulkner showed his hand,
He thought that by internment he could break our rebel band.
But the boys from Ballymurphy, how they showed the way that night
When they taught those English soldiers how Irish men can fight.

Provo politics

The violence was about politics as well as psychology. Certainly, the Provisionals had created an extraordinary level of mayhem. Had the nationalist population of Northern Ireland been in the majority, it can hardly be doubted that a British withdrawal would have been forced. But it was not so simple, and nimble footwork was required of the Provos. In August 1971, with the introduction of internment, they issued five ceasefire demands and called for the release of all 'political prisoners', an end to Stormont, and compensation to the victims of British army violence. Crucially they included demands for the legalization of Sinn Féin and freedom for elections to Dáil Uladh.

The IRA had fought an effective war in 1919–21 because it could plausibly claim to represent a morally and democratically valid entity: Dáil Eireann. From the moment British troops were deployed in 1969, the British government had been careful to stress that only the Northern Ireland state, as set by the 1920 Government of Ireland Act, could give consent to dissolution of the Union. By definition, Northern Ireland could never constitute a community challenging the British connection.

The crisis in the north failed to ignite the island of Ireland, and thus there was insufficient pressure to recreate this as the unit of self-determination. A revolutionary Dáil Eireann could not be reborn. The Provos' political strategy hazily acknowledged this harsh reality. They proposed a nine-county Ulster assembly—Dáil Uladh—as a constituent of a federal island free from British interference, Eire Nua (New Ireland). This had a certain plausibility; it was conceivable that a radicalized organization of the nine counties' Catholics, who were in a bare majority, might have acted as a counterweight to the Stormont system, now boycotted by nationalist representatives. Had Dáil Uladh taken off, the naturalness of the six-county state would have been called into question.

Constitional nationalists refused to play along, however, and the government of the Republic was loath to have its Ulster territory embroiled. Above all, however, the Provos were insufficiently politically mature to hold back their military activities to the degree necessary to establish a quasi-state capable of challenging the legitimacy of Northern Ireland. They slipped into the fantasy of militarism itself being sufficient to weary Britain of its commitment to Ulster's unionists. Said Provo chief of staff Sean MacStiofain in early 1972:

People say, if the British army is withdrawn from the North there'll be a Protestant backlash. We've been blackmailed with this threat for years. If it comes to it, we'll have to deal with it, we don't want it, but the best defence against it is a strong IRA. I don't think it would be a lasting thing—it would come and go and that would be that. . . . I can't see these people preparing themselves for a protracted guerrilla war. It's just not in them. What I think you would see if there was a declaration of intent to withdraw by the British, would be an exodus of the more bigoted elements in the North. . . . There would be no place for those who say they want their British heritage. They've got to accept their Irish heritage, and the Irish way of life, no matter who they are, otherwise there would be no place for them. . . . We say, the armed struggle comes first, then you politicise . . . we've no doubt that military victory is within our grasp.

Thus a set of ceasefire proposals issued in March 1972 dropped the demand for freedom for electoral agitation. The hope now was for both 'belligerent armies' to negotiate directly, as military men. To indicate their own discipline, the IRA called a 72-hour truce.

As Northern Ireland teetered on the brink of civil war in March 1972 the Conservative government suspended Northern Ireland's devolved government. The fall of Stormont was a major victory in the Provos' campaign to delegitimize the Northern Ireland state. A secretary of state for Northern Ireland now sat in the United Kingdom cabinet and acted as a semi-colonial governor. Such was the determination to rule even-handedly if non-democratically, even junior ministers were drawn from British constituencies. William Whitelaw, the first 'direct ruler', attempted to recruit a local advisory commission, but this was no more than a token. Brian Faulkner, displaced Northern Ireland prime minister, sourly criticized the province's demotion to the status of 'a coconut colony'.

In this context, the IRA leadership on 22 June 1972 announced plans for a seven-day ceasefire to begin on 26 June at midnight, provided that the British government agreed to do the same, and invited Secretary of State Whitelaw to meet them directly. Whitelaw responded in parliament by saying that if the IRA called for a ceasefire, 'Her Majesty's forces will obviously reciprocate'. On 7 July MacStiofain and the other representatives, including the young Gerry Adams, specifically released from Long Kesh for the purpose, were flown to London for a meeting with Whitelaw. The IRA delegation stated their demand that 'the British government recognise publicly that it is the right of the people of Ireland acting as a unit to decide the future of Ireland'. Given a certain IRA flexibility already indicated by Dáil Uladh, this was not quite as unyielding as it might have seemed. Britain, however, despite its abolition of the old Stormont system, had settled on copper-fastening the six-county state as the basis of consent. Space was left for further negotiation, but on 9 July, in the course of a three-way clash between the IRA, UDA, and British army in the Lenadoon housing estate in Belfast, the truce broke down. The IRA's political opportunity, such as it was, had passed.

The Provos reverted to militarism, deploying with increasing ruthlessness the car bomb. On 21 July 1972, in the space of an hour, 22 bombs detonated in Belfast, killing nine. At a time when television coverage spared viewers little, the image of dismembered bodies being shovelled into bin bags induced revulsion. The IRA's insistence that civilians must bear the collateral costs of their campaign was shaken by such a visceral atrocity. Much moral capital the IRA had accumulated through relatively selective targeting, British errors such as Bloody Sunday, and carefully timed ceasefires and policy initiatives, was wasted. Determined to limit the IRA's capacity, and capitalizing on its crisis of legitimacy, the government sent the army back into no-go areas, notably the Bogside in Derry, on 31 July (Operation Motorman). For this they employed 26,000 soldiers, along with tanks, bulldozers, Saracens, and helicopters—the biggest British military operation since Suez. For the IRA, illusions of a quick victory evaporated.

Loyalists

For a period the threat of republican victory looked very real to Protestants. Vanguard, an organization led by former Stormont minister of home affairs Bill Craig, attracted a mass following. Tens of thousands attended its militaristic rallies, to hear Craig spit threats. 'We must build up a dossier of the men and women who are a menace to this country', he told one such gathering on 18 March 1972, 'because if and when the politicians fail us, it may be our job to liquidate the

enemy.' This may have been bluster, but the loyalist hard-
men were prepared for grimly real deeds.

Loyalist paramilitaries entered the fray of sectarian assassination in late 1970, upping the ante ferociously from the
collapse of Stormont in 1972. By the end of the year, 80
Catholic civilians had been assassinated. These attacks were
not claimed by any organization, but in fact there was motive
and direction behind them. The Ulster Defence Association
(UDA) was primarily responsible. Formed in September
1971 from a number of loyalist vigilante groups, it was heavily implicated in intimidation of hundreds of Catholic families from mixed and Protestant areas. From the imposition
of direct rule in March 1972, the UDA participated in an
assassination campaign against civilian Catholics. At first
attacks were not claimed, but from 1973 the UDA adopted
the *nom de guerre* of Ulster Freedom Fighters (UFF). The
UDA was only declared illegal in 1992. It attracted many
thousands of members (at its peak the estimated membership was 40,000) and very quickly became a formidable
force, particularly in Belfast. Smaller was the Ulster Volunteer Force (dating from 1966), though it exhibited some
greater degree of discipline and sophistication.

The overt sectarianism of loyalist violence had a significant
purchase on unionist tradition. Anti-catholicism was historically central to unionist psychology, in contrast to the
avowal, indeed insistence, of nationalists and republicans
that all inhabitants of the island, Catholic and Protestant,
were part of the nation (whether they wished to be or not).
Protestants, however, considered that catholicism was an

autocratic belief system, superstitious and conspiratorial. It made Catholic Ireland effete and inferior. In 1964, for example, John Brooke, son of Prime Minister Lord Brookeborough and later a Unionist MP, explained that: 'The leopard does not change his spots. The Roman Catholic Church demands loyalty to the Church, which modifies loyalty to the state. . . . Our discrimination is not against Roman Catholics. We are trying to prevent the Roman Catholic Church in its determination to destroy Ulster.' Ian Paisley, a fundamentalist cleric given to raging against the 'Romish whore' and 'anti-christ' (the Pope), was throughout the Troubles the single most popular unionist politician. In this context, it is little surprise that virulent sectarianism could tip over into murderous rage.

There was much more than unthinking sectarian animus to loyalism, however. Loyalist violence raged incessantly throughout the period of constitutional uncertainty, until the Callagan Labour government of 1977–9 ruled out further political innovation and concentrated on bearing down on republican terrorism within the context of stabilized direct rule. The state in Northern Ireland had always massively armed its Protestant population, as much to canalize potential vigilantism as to control nationalist irredentism. From 1969 the British army shouldered the burden. The army (and later other legal military forces—the RUC, Ulster Defence Regiment/Royal Irish Rangers) was sufficient focus for Protestant martial honour. Loyalist paramilitaries were thus unable as effectively as the IRA to act as legitimizers of communal identity and pride. Loyalists knew they were

9 Ulster Defence Association parade outside Belfast City Hall, 27 May 1972. The UDA was the largest single paramilitary in Northern Ireland, yet its political voice was mute and it never seriously challenged the grip of the mainstream unionist parties

fighting a dark, largely unheroic war, directed against defenceless civilians. It may have been, in their thinking, necessary, but it was not worthy. When the Combined Loyalist Military Command declared their ceasefire in October 1994, they expressed 'abject and true remorse' for their depredations (but did not repudiate them). This would have been unthinkable for republicans.

However, they gained support, or at least tolerance, as unofficial and self-appointed state adjuncts, carrying war to the knife and transcending the excessively limiting rules of engagement imposed on state forces. Their actions, not symbolic of national pride but politically and militarily calculated to suppress nationalist insurgency, were deliberately outrageous—usually targeting civilians expressly—and in this regard can be differentiated from typical republican operations. Loyalist violence seemed to glory in its barbarity. Torture-murders were not unusual. The 'romper room', where victims were ritually tortured, was a feature of many loyalist drinking dens. One particular gang, the Shankill Butchers, so called for their use of butchers' knives, killed at least 19 people in the 1970s. Such murders cannot merely be dismissed as the act of psychotics. Over the Troubles almost 700 Catholic civilians died at loyalist hands (plus over 100 Protestants, often taken for Catholics—the largest single category of victim. The aim of loyalist violence was to impress upon Britain and Irish nationalism that political appeasement of republicanism was not a violence-free option.

Certainly, such savagery owed something to the typical elements from which loyalism drew its recruits. Those wishing to fight a respectable war had a range of legitimate security forces they could join. Many Protestants fought their war with distinction and honour in the security forces. It is true that loyalists liked to consider themselves as adjuncts to the state, and there is evidence of collaboration between legal and illegal forces through the Troubles. Hundreds of security-force members, principally from the Ulster Defence Regiment, a locally recruited unit of the British army, overwhelmingly Protestant, have been convicted for collusion.

However, the security services consistently had a much higher rate of arrest against loyalists than nationalists. Sentences were not noticeably lighter. Loyalist paramilitaries were not simply government-run death squads.

Loyalists were often drunk when on operations. However, there was method to their superficially lumpen violence. First, they hoped to terrorize the IRA civilian 'support base'. As Gusty Spence, the UVF's veteran leader, put it, 'if it wasn't possible to get at the IRA then some thought, "We'll get those who are harbouring them, succouring them, comforting them and supporting them".' Secondly, they wanted to indicate the lengths to which Protestant militants would go in the event of a 'doomsday' situation. British withdrawal would lead not to Protestant acquiescence, but to a bloodbath.

There is no doubt that loyalism attracted a fair degree of support on this basis. An admittedly imprecise telephone poll in 1993 found that 42 per cent supported loyalist paramilitary violence, and 81 per cent stated that loyalist violence was a reaction to the IRA's campaign. Mainstream unionists abhor this violence, but have conceded that it served a cause, if immorally. Said John Taylor, a Unionist MP, of the assassination of Catholics in 1993, 'in a perverse way this is something which may be helpful because they . . . [Catholics] . . . are now beginning to appreciate more clearly the fear that has existed within the Protestant community for the past twenty years as they have been killed at random by the IRA.'*

* *Irish News*, 9 September 1993.

The loyalist utilitarian view of violence and the essentially reactive nature of loyalism belie loyalists' assumed political extremism. They are constitutional conservatives, not neo-fascist radicals—thus the ostensibly surprising moderation of loyalist political wings, the Ulster Democratic Party (UDP—connected to the UVF) and Popular Unionist Party (PUP—connected to the UDA) that emerged in the 1990s. Loyalism gives a glimpse of what reasonable men and women will turn to if they consider their existence as a people to be in danger.

Conclusion

Most Protestants did not accept the claims of the civil rights movement that it wished merely for the rights of British citizens. Determined to expose its nationalist character, a substantial minority instinctively set siege to Catholics, corralling them physically and politically. This in turn detonated a nationalist reaction from Catholics. Increasingly the British government and army, seeking merely to keep peace and reform the state, were sucked into the dynamic of polarization.

The Catholic revolt was exploited by the IRA, a tiny organization in 1969, but drawing upon powerfully evocative traditions. It had a coherent belief system that, in denying the right of democratic opinion to override nationalist ideals of an independent united Ireland, immunized it from public censure. Its theology perfectly suited a revolutionary elitist

organization. Without mass British army repression, however, inspired by a simplistic militarism, it could never have
grown to its powerful position.

All-Ireland nationalism felt itself on the brink of a historic
breakthrough. The southern elite expressed its conviction
that Northern Ireland was a failed entity. 'The division
of Ireland has never been, and is not now, acceptable to
the great majority of the Irish people', said Jack Lynch, the
Republic's Taoiseach in August 1971. It joined with the
political representatives of Northern Ireland's Catholics,
the SDLP, to demand the abolition of Stormont and the
renegotiation of partition.

The fall of Stormont in March 1972, to be replaced by
direct rule from Britain, escalated Protestant fears of a sell-
out. Loyalist violence soared to indicate that the ability to
disrupt ordinary life lay not only with the IRA. Moderate
nationalist opinion drew back, and increasingly accepted
that which Britain had insisted since Prime Minister Harold
Wilson's Downing Street Declaration of August 1969 (to
steady nerves after furious rioting), that only Northern
Ireland could determine for itself whether the union with
Britain be ended. In the long run this historically strengthened unionism. Its legitimacy shifted away from control of
Storment, morally compromised by one-party rule, to the
will of the numerical majority within the six counties of
Northern Ireland. Instability remained, however, because
of massive nationalist alienation and unionist fears that a
disgruntled Britain would acquiesce in undermining the
union by degrees.

4

The Long War

Constitutional politics

As poll evidence consistently indicated, Catholics broadly speaking were prepared to countenance a political settlement well short of a united, independent Ireland. Moreover, Catholics were confident that inexorable processes of demographic movement and the diminishing of borders in an integrated Europe would lead to communal Catholic victory. The relative moderation of Catholic political perspective was at odds with the widespread sympathy for armed struggle.

By far the largest nationalist political vehicle was the SDLP. Formed on 21 August 1970 from a clutch of independent Stormont MPs, its first leader was the left-leaning Belfast politician Gerry Fitt. The SDLP absorbed much of the traditional Nationalist Party support, but hoped to transcend its sterile focus on the 'border question' by emphasizing social and economic questions. It stood for eventual Irish unity by agreement. Certainly it came under pressure from republicanism, and reacted negatively by withdrawing from the local Stormont parliament in protest at British army repression and later the introduction of internment. Its emphasis on winning Protestant consent weakened when in September 1972 it proposed a form of joint sovereignty by the British and Irish governments over Northern Ireland.

The failure of the IRA to develop a credible political strategy, however, allowed the SDLP to easily regain the initiative. When the Provos suggested talks with Secretary of State Whitelaw in June 1971, they believed they could imperiously by-pass outmoded elected politicians. Whitelaw rejected the offer, but the IRA's move allowed the SDLP to get itself off a hook. It had refused to talk with the government while internment remained. Now that the IRA had ignored this stipulation, SDLP members felt able to break the crippling embargo themselves. They suggested to Whitelaw that he take up the IRA's offer and, probably somewhat to their consternation, Whitelaw agreed. The talks led nowhere, however, and the Provos had inadvertently rehabilitated political dialogue. In truth, most Catholics appreciated that IRA militarism might have a defensive function, and more again thrilled at its sheer élan. But it was not seen as a credible political vehicle.

Sunningdale

Britain stridently reaffirmed its defence of the Northern Ireland state as the only basis for self-determination. This was clear in *Northern Ireland: Constitutional Proposals*, issued in March 1973. It reaffirmed 'that Northern Ireland will remain part of the United Kingdom for as long as that is the wish of a majority of its people'. The IRA was firmly excluded from formal politics: 'small but dangerous minorities which would seek to impose their views by violence and coercion' would not 'be allowed to participate in working institutions they wish to destroy'. More strikingly, even peaceful abstention from the institutions of partition would rule republicans out of negotiations. Only those who were prepared to 'seek the unification of Ireland by consent' and were 'genuinely prepared to work for the welfare of Northern Ireland' were offered 'the opportunity to play no less a part in the life and public affairs of Northern Ireland than is open to their fellow citizens'. Those who refused to acknowledge the six counties as a fair basis for national self-determination were barred.

To reinforce the point, only those willing to participate in elections to a new Northern Ireland Assembly, elected as soon as possible by proportional representation, would be admitted to negotiations with the secretary of state. This was impossible for the republican movement—despite Britain's previous acknowledgement that it enjoyed a 'considerable degree of mass support'—for ideological reasons and because Sinn Féin, its political wing, was illegal. The aim, explicitly, was a new devolved government for Northern Ireland. However, devolved government would not be acceptable to Britain if 'solely based upon any single party, if that party draws its support and its elected representation virtually entirely from only one section of a divided community'. There was, however, a concession to nationalist conceptions of the 'Irish dimension': 'The Government favours, and is prepared to facilitate, the establishment of institutional arrangements for consultation and co-operation between Northern Ireland and the Republic of Ireland.' This was enough to entice the SDLP into negotiations in 1973.

Unionism was less amenable. The Ulster Unionist Party had boycotted British officials since the fall of Stormont, but now its leader, Brian Faulkner, steered it back in from the wilderness. The governing body of the party, the Ulster Unionist Council, voted by 381 to 231 votes to enter negotiations on the basis of the white paper. However, the party split and in the subsequent assembly elections 26 Unionists returned were explicitly opposed to its proposals. Fifty-two seats were held by all parties prepared to negotiate.

The new assembly met amidst rowdy scenes. In November 1973 three parties, the UUP, SDLP, and moderate Alliance Party, agreed to form a power-sharing executive to govern Northern Ireland. The executive was to consist of eleven members: six Faulknerite Unionists, four SDLP, and one Alliance Party of Northern Ireland (APNI). There were also to be four non-executive office holders who would not have a vote: two SDLP, one Unionist, and one Alliance Party. The Irish dimension had yet to be sorted out, however, and to this end, in December 1973, the parties met at Sunningdale, a civil-service training centre in Britain. This was the first tripartite meeting between the governments of Britain, southern Ireland, and Northern Ireland since 1925. A Council of Ireland was finally agreed. This was to consist of a council of ministers, upon which both Irish governments would be represented equally, and which was to have an 'executive and harmonizing' function. A supplementary consultative assembly would bring together 30 members from the Northern Ireland Assembly and the same number from the Dáil.

The new coalition took office on 1 January 1974. The power-sharing government worked moderately well, but Sunningdale proved altogether contentious. Early in January 1974 the Ulster Unionist Council voted, by 427 votes to 374, to reject the Council of Ireland, and Brian Faulkner was forced to resign the leadership of his party, though he still had an assembly majority as head of the power-sharing executive. His attempts to pitch Sunningdale as simply an agreement between two neighbouring governments was weakened when an SDLP assemblyman, in a speech at Trinity College Dublin, described the Council of Ireland as 'the vehicle that would trundle Unionists into a united Ireland'.

This basic inability of the pro-agreement parties to agree on its significance meant that an electoral pact was impossible. All constitutional parties opposed to the pact were unionist, and they had no such difficulty in uniting. Their opportunity came in February 1974, when British domestic circumstances demanded a United Kingdom general election, no matter how inopportune for Northern Ireland. Three main loyalist parties formed the anti-Sunningdale United Ulster Unionist Council (UUUC): the Democratic Unionist Party (DUP), led by Ian Paisley; (Ulster) Vanguard, led by William Craig; and the Official Unionists (OUP), led by Harry West. Their slogan was, 'Dublin is just a Sunningdale away'. Candidates standing on behalf of the UUUC won eleven of the twelve Northern Ireland seats, gaining 51.1 per cent of the valid votes. The SDLP held West Belfast.

The assembly and executive remained and functioned, however. This body was due for re-election in 1976, by which time it was hoped that power sharing would have bedded down and gained in popularity. However, when on 14 May 1974 a motion put to the assembly condemning power sharing and the Council of Ireland was defeated by 44 votes to 28, the loyalist Ulster Worker's Council announced a protest general strike.

Most expected this to be something of a damp squib. Andy Tyrie, commander of the UDA, told his brigade staff that there was insufficient support for a spontaneously successful stoppage: 'It's going to be up to us to do the dirty work again.' Indeed, massive intimidation was primarily responsible for the strike's effectiveness in the early days. However, as the loyalist workers proved themselves a power in the land, power and fuel shortages jammed up the entire provincial economy. Protestants began to rally to their cause. Few were prepared to stand by power sharing and particularly the hated Council of Ireland. An attempt on Tuesday 21 May by Len Murray, the general secretary of the Trades Union Council, to lead a 'back-to-work' march was a fiasco. The SDLP unwillingly agreed to postpone certain sections of the Sunningdale agreement until 1977 and to reduce the size of the Council of Ireland. Momentum had built up, however. The new Labour secretary of state, Merlyn Rees, felt little personal investment in the dispute and did not trust the civil service, RUC, or army to cooperate in a heavy-handed approach to the strikers. Pressure for action from the Republic's government was tempered by two loyalist car bombs in Dublin and Monaghan, Republic of Ireland, in which 33 people died (the highest toll during any single day of the Troubles).

In a television broadcast on 25 May, Harold Wilson, British prime minister, gave vent to his long-standing irritation with the expense and bother of his country's Ulster citizens:

> The people on this side of the water—British parents—have seen their sons vilified and spat upon and murdered. British taxpayers have seen the taxes they have poured out, almost without regard to cost—over £300 million a year this year the cost of the Army operation on top of that—going into Northern Ireland. They see property destroyed by evil violence and are asked to pick up the bill for rebuilding it. Yet people who benefit from all this now viciously defy Westminster, purporting to act as though they were an elected government; people who spend their lives sponging on Westminster and British democracy and then systematically assault democratic methods. Who do these people think they are? It is when we see the kind of arrogant, undemocratic behaviour now going on that the patience of citizens, parents, taxpayers becomes strained.

The derisive response of many Protestants the following day was to pin twists of sponge to their lapel.

With the prospect of an almost complete power black-out, and the failure of even basic sanitary systems, the crisis came to a head on 28 May, day fourteen of the strike. Brian Faulkner demanded that negotiations be opened with the

UWC. Merlyn Rees, the secretary of state, was adamant that bodies outside the assembly could not be formally treated with. Faulkner and his Unionist colleagues on the executive resigned and the entire power-sharing settlement, stripped of any cross-community credibility, promptly collapsed.

Ulsterization

Direct rule was resumed. The government sharply reversed from its strategy of excluding the extremes, and lifted the ban on Sinn Féin and the UVF (the UDA was already legal) in the hope that the 'extremists' could reimagine the partition settlement. Rees held out some hope for an independent Northern Ireland as a precursor to an all-Ireland federal solution. He was not prepared to coerce, however, and the Constitutional Convention elected in 1975 was dominated not by 'creative' extremists, but the recalcitrant Ulster Unionist Party, stripped of its moderates, and an embittered SDLP. Politics was at an impasse. On the unionist side, a blank refusal to consider power sharing or an Irish dimension. On the Catholic side, insistence upon power sharing and an Irish dimension. Britain did not feel inclined to force the issue with either.

Provisions were made to adjust direct rule for the long haul. Northern Ireland 'orders' were given a little more time for oversight at Westminster and the number of Ulster MPs at Westminster was increased from twelve to eighteen. The regime remained, however, quasi-colonial.

Since Operation Motorman, the republican movement had drifted into something of a strategic impasse. Their success rate in 1973 and 1974 fell dramatically as British army saturation policing winkled out valuable intelligence, and the Northern Ireland (Emergency Provisions) Act of that year abolished jury trials for terrorist offences, making convictions easier to secure. Increasing emphasis was laid on covert security operations, a grim war of the shadows. In 1972 the Military Reconnaissance Force (MRF) was created to combine 'intelligence gathering' with 'aggressive patrolling' within the republican areas. This was supplemented with a panoply of 'psychological warfare' units, such as NITAT (Northern Ireland Training Team) and the 14th Intelligence Unit.

The use of undercover operatives, in a shady semi-legal world, gave rise to a stream of lurid 'dirty war' allegations. British state involvement was alleged in two car bombs that exploded in Dublin on 1 December 1972, killing two civilians, as the Dublin parliament was deliberating on anti-terrorist legislation. Two days into the Ulster Workers strike against Sunningdale in 1974, loyalist paramilitaries exploded car bombs in Dublin and Monaghan, killing 33 civilians. The Irish police, seeming to catch wind of the involvement of perhaps rogue elements of British security, quickly wound up the inconclusive investigation.

The security drive against the IRA was effective. In 1973 eighty security personnel were killed, in 1974 52. Well aware that British interest in the Northern Ireland conflict was diminishing, the IRA cast round for new forms of 'armed

10 Civilian searched by army. In the 1970s civilian life in many urban areas was seriously inconvenienced by an obtrusive security presence. It felt like a society at war

propaganda'. They fixed on attacks within Great Britain itself. Notoriously, 5 people were killed and 44 injured in a pub bombing in Guildford on 5 October 1974. The following month 19 died and 182 were wounded in Birmingham. Certainly this did refocus British attention, but mainly to the detriment of innocent Irishmen picked up, brutalized, and unjustly imprisoned. The Guildford Four and Birmingham Six became *causes célèbres*, only winning their release in the 1990s. Ironically, this piling of tragedy upon tragedy did something to convert the appalling atrocities of the pub bombings into propaganda boons for the republican movement.

Truce

In the aftermath of Sunningdale, Secretary of State Merlyn Rees toyed with the idea of drawing in the paramilitaries to hammer out a solution. To this end the UVF and Sinn Féin were legalized. Republicans saw some scope for hope and in January 1975 the Provisional IRA announced a Christmas truce after talks with Protestant churchmen. It lasted until 16 January. Loyalists were unimpressed, and after an upsurge of assassination, the UVF was once more proscribed in October. The IRA, however, was convinced that, with the failure of Sunningdale, Britain must be considering withdrawal. The government, in secret contacts, did little to disabuse them of the notion.

The IRA thus entered into an open-ended 'truce' on 10 February 1975. Britain reciprocated by opening seven 'incident centres', manned by members of Sinn Féin who liaised with government officials at the Northern Ireland office. The army even supplied green Ford Cortinas in which Provisionals could patrol openly, easily recognizable to British troops. As the Provos were strung along, with little sign of political advance, their discipline began to deteriorate. There were numerous operations by IRA units in the border area and some even in Belfast. The truce was brought to an effective end by the Derry IRA, who, having always been opposed to the truce, decided to blow up the town's joint incident centre.

The truce in some form technically lasted into January 1976. It did little to damp down violence, but its nature warped towards that of the gang-land. The Provos feuded with the still intact Official IRA, coming off rather worse. More seriously, frightened by apparent republican confidence that British withdrawal was pending, loyalists escalated their assassination campaign. The truce had been secretly negotiated by MI6 in the aftermath of the Birmingham pub bombings. The army were furious that secret talks were being held with the IRA, believing that they had the IRA 'on the run'. Suspicions existed that disaffected agents, and members of the locally recruited and largely Protestant RUC and Ulster Defence Regiment (UDR), gave succour to loyalist assassins. Certainly there were proven incidents of collusion at the level of individual members of the security forces. Loyalist killings of civilians increased from 87 in 1974, to 96 in 1975, to a peak of 110 in 1976. The IRA carried out 'retaliatory' sectarian murders. On 4 January the Protestant Action Force (PAF) killed five Catholics in South Armagh. The next day the IRA took ten Protestant civilians off a bus at Kingsmill, South Armagh, and killed them.

This created ideal conditions for the government to 'criminalize' the conflict. The IRA were redefined as lawless bandits. William Whitelaw had already reduced, largely for political reasons, the blanket harassment of Catholic areas. With a more strategic eye, Merlyn Rees continued on this

11 Waterfront Hall, Lanyon Place. By the 1970s and 1980s declining violence and massive state spending did much to 'normalize' civilian life. Prestige projects were designed to attract favourable press and lure visitors to Northern Ireland

track. In 1975 he commissioned a report, *The Way Ahead*, that decisively rejected the counter-insurgency strategy still advocated by the army, in favour of an internal security strategy. This involved the so-called Ulsterization of the conflict by means of two related policies: criminalization and police primacy.

The army was to be relieved of overall responsibility for the campaign against the Provisional IRA, which would become instead a law-and-order matter to be handled by the RUC with the support of the army. Under an English officer, Kenneth Newman, the new chief constable from 1976, the RUC was reorganized into an efficient force, heavily armed but striving for the norms of non-military policing. There was an element of artifice to all this. The Bennet Report of 1979 confirmed suspicions that forced confessions were regularly being accepted as uncorroborated evidence by Diplock (non-jury) courts.

Following the Kingsmill massacre, Harold Wilson announced that 150 SAS soldiers would be sent to Armagh, 'bandit country'. By March 1976 the SAS had begun a series of covert operations aimed at disrupting the IRA command structure. On 12 March 1976 they abducted a member of the IRA, Sean McKenna, from his house in the Irish Republic. On 15 April the SAS shot another member of the IRA, Peter Cleary. An anonymous SAS officer told *The Guardian* in late 1976: 'We were all very enthusiastic about going and wasting a few of the IRA.' With the development of a new military strategy against the IRA and the end of constitutional innovation, the loyalist assassinations dropped off, from 110 in

1976 to 19 in 1977, 6 in 1978, and 12 in 1979. A loyalist strike in May 1977 supported by Ian Paisley demanding a tougher state response against the IRA similarly flopped. Few believed that the government now was prepared to 'sell out' to the IRA, and its hard-nosed security policies appeared adequate.

Rees's successor, Roy Mason, was soon publicly boasting that victory was around the corner. Security forces were less sanguine, however. The IRA adapted to the end of mass membership (from thousands to a regular cadre of maybe 300 to 500) and relatively large-scale, low-tech confrontations with the security forces by adopting a cellular structure. A military intelligence report, written in 1978, concluded:

> Our evidence of the calibre of rank and file terrorists does not support the view that they are mindless hooligans drawn from the unemployed and the employable . . . The Provisional IRA will probably continue to recruit the men it needs. They will still be able to attract enough people with leadership talent, good education and manual skills to continue to enhance their all round professionalism. The movement will retain popular support sufficient to maintain secure bases in the traditional republican areas.

The IRA held its own. It was still capable of frightful triumphs. On 27 August 1979, for example, the aged Lord Mountbatten and three others were killed by the Provisional IRA whilst sailing. On the same day, an IRA bomb trap in County Down killed eighteen soldiers. But mass confrontations in Belfast and Derry had ended, partly a function of pressure from the security forces, partly of a demarcation of antagonistic communities. There were now few mixed working-class areas. IRA operations were now much more classically 'terrorist'. They lacked the heroic immediacy of massed firefights. A one-time volunteer, Sean O'Callaghan, recalled with revulsion the cold-bloodedness of one such hit:

Peter Flanagan was at the bar reading the *Irish Independent.* He understood what was happening and began to move from his stool. 'No, please, No!' I steadied, took aim and fired. He was still moving, trying to escape. He stumbled to the door leading to the toilets and fell through it. I fired eight times and knew that most, if not all, of my shots had hit him.

Such tactics seemed to promise no quick breakthrough. In this context it is little wonder that rumblings for peace amongst Catholics in particular rose to a brief roar. In August 1976 IRA gunmen engaged the British army from a speeding car—a classic 'scoot' operation—in Anderstown, Belfast. The army responded, shooting dead the driver. Out of control, the vehicle careered into a group of pedestrians and three children from the same family were killed. This sparked, for a few brief months, a substantial peace movement. Mairead Corrigan (an aunt of the victims), Betty Williams, and the journalist Ciaran McKeown organized a series of peace marches attracting tens of thousands. Catholics and Protestants symbolically joined to walk both the Falls and the Shankill Road in Belfast. However, an unwillingness to equate state with paramilitary violence led to a falling off of support from Catholics, the credibility of the peace movement being further undermined by unseemly squabbling over the disposal of the Nobel Peace Prize money it won in 1976.

Britain's abandonment of constitutional innovation and 'low-intensity war' in favour of direct rule and 'Ulsterization' of the conflict paid security dividends. In 1972, the peak year for violence in Northern Ireland, there were 496 deaths, 258 of them civilian. This fell to 263 in 1973, rose to over 300 in 1974, fell again to 206 in 1975, and rose to 308 in 1976. Thereafter, however, the death rate hovered around the 80 to 110 range. Mass communal violence had largely died down, the IRA was restricted in its operations, and, until the later 1980s, loyalist violence fell off dramatically. The war, however, dragged on.

Though the truce had weakened the IRA, it may have been a tactical error by the British. By stringing the organization along, it resurrected fears of British perfidy. Hopes were raised of tangible constitutional concessions that may well have allowed the IRA to abandon its campaign without loss of face, but no such concessions were made. The problem was that, for sections of the alienated Catholic working class, 'resistance' was an end in itself, a badge of military pride and a guarantee against assimilation into a non-Irish identity. One could not be mistaken for British whilst at the same time levying war against Britain.

The IRA came close to defeat during the 1975 truce, but having reached an early peak, they could now draw upon momentum. With the onset of communal violence, Catholics had looked to the IRA for self-defence. The IRA historically nurtured an ideology that equated national pride with a willingness to take to arms. British army militarization, visited upon the Catholic ghettos, seemed to validate this military victory. Even after the end of the Provos' 'heroic' phase, loyalty and pride in the 'people's army' ensured a significant support base for a rationalized IRA cadre to continue its campaign. It found itself in the murderous cul de sac of equating continued resistance with an ongoing moral victory.

Some more constructive institutional defence of the Irish Catholic identity was necessary to render nugatory the Provos' 'long war'.

The hunger strikes

The Conservatives appeared to favour the entrenchment of direct rule ideologically as well as pragmatically, and before their election in 1979 espoused merely a shadowy regional council or councils to temper direct rule. In power, however, the Conservatives switched to a concentration on co-operation with the Republic of Ireland. In December 1980 there was a high-level summit in Dublin between British and Irish ministers, and in 1981 a formal Anglo-Irish Intergovernmental Council was created. Nor was devolution ignored, though 'rolling devolution', the election in 1982 of an assembly to which powers might be allocated piecemeal as and when agreement was arrived at, never developed further than a talking shop. The SDLP were unwilling to play footsie with unionists prepared only to offer much less than had been in place in 1974, and they boycotted proceedings.

Impetus for something more radical came, ironically, from the very attempt by the British to create quasi-normal conditions of direct rule in Northern Ireland in the late 1970s. Led by Billy McKee, a senior Belfast Provisional, 40 republican prisoners had embarked upon a hunger strike in 1972, demanding POW status. An erroneous rumour that McKee had died sparked rioting in Belfast and the hunger strike ended after 37 days when government, anxious not to derail talks, agreed to grant the prisoners what it termed 'special category status'. In 1975, however, the Labour government decided to phase out the 'special status' designation. IRA prisoners were to be treated no longer as de facto POWs, but as common criminals. This was a piece of the overall strategy to recast the conflict as primarily a law-and-order crisis. The RUC would take the lead in anti-terrorist activity, special legislation would be phased out, and 'normalization' of direct rule would take precedence over political initiatives.

On 16 September 1976, Ciaran Nugent was brought into the Long Kesh (renamed the Maze) prison, having been convicted of a terrorist offence that occurred after 1 March 1976, the cut-off date for special category status. When offered a prison uniform, he refused to accept it. Naked, he wrapped himself in his prison bedding. By late 1980, approximately 340 prisoners were 'on the blanket'.

In a closed and fevered atmosphere, bitter attrition with the hard-nosed prison authorities escalated the republican

12 The first hunger striker to die, Bobby Sands calculated on self-sacrifice. He became the IRA's best-known icon

non-cooperation campaign into dramatic, even grotesque forms. In 1978 there evolved the 'no wash protest', followed by the 'dirty protest', in which prisoners smeared their cells with their excrement rather than attend to prison rules in visiting the toilet facilities. Rarely was the republican slogan—'For those who understand, no explanation is necessary, for those who do not understand, no explanation is possible'—more relevant.

The IRA Army Council was reluctant to permit a hunger strike, for fear of demoralization were it to be faced down. The prisoners, locked in an intense battle of wills, insisted, however, and in October of 1980, permission was granted to escalate. A total of 33 prisoners participated in the hunger strike, including one female (Mairéad Farrell, in 1988 to be controversially gunned down whilst on a bombing mission in Gibraltar). Before any died, however, the strike was called off when the prisoners interpreted a British offer of 'civilian-type clothing' as granting them de facto political status. When it became clear that it was no such thing a new hunger strike was launched on 1 March 1981, the fifth anniversary of the abolition of special category status.

The prisoners' rationale cut clear to their self-perception as a legitimate army: 'We, the Republican Prisoners of War in the H-Blocks, Long Kesh, demand, as of right, political recognition and that we be accorded the status of political prisoners. We claim this right as captured combatants in the continuing struggle for national liberation and self-determination.' It is noteworthy that the tradition of republican painted murals, usually on gable walls in Catholic working-class areas, dates from this time. Certainly the hunger strikes were a major theme of the murals, but they were depicted not as a humanitarian issue, calculated to appeal to moderate opinion, but closely in conjunction with the theme of 'armed struggle'.

Margaret Thatcher, the British prime minister, agreed that this was not primarily a dispute over the humanity of prison conditions, but the legitimacy of IRA violence. She responded determinedly that: 'There is no such thing as political murder, political bombing or political violence. There is only criminal murder, criminal bombing and criminal violence. We will not compromise on this. There will be no political status.' However, the prisoners' specific demands—that they not be required to wear a prison uniform or do prison work and that they be allowed to associate freely with other prisoners, organize their own educational and recreational facilities, and have one visit, one letter, and one parcel per week—attracted much Catholic and indeed international sympathy on civil libertarian grounds. To capitalize on the massive upsurge of sympathy the hunger strikers received, the prisoners explicitly stated that they were happy for their five demands to be applied to all convicts, politically motivated or not. They denied that this was a concession on principle, but in diluting their demands for particular rights as POWs, it was.

Murals

Loyalist murals have a long tradition. Orange imagery migrated from elaborate banners to gable walls around the time of the third home rule crisis (1912–14). At first they depicted traditional Orange imagery, especially King William (Billy), upon his white charger, victorious over the Catholic King James in 1690. During the Stormont years, dignitaries of the governing party were often present at the unveiling of new murals.

Following direct rule, loyalist mural painting declined. The tradition was reinvigorated from the republican side, when

13 A Loyalist King Billy mural

murals, often celebrating the exploits of the IRA, appeared from the time of the 1981 hunger strikes. Loyalist mural painting revived, particularly from the time of the Anglo-Irish Agreement, and echoed republican militarism. They were much more overtly anti-Catholic than hitherto. With the peace process of the 1990s, however, the murals became rather less violence-orientated, notably on the republican side, instead often articulating quite complex political messages.

14 IRA mural

Murals are now executed with some professionalism, and even if they lack the old spontaneity, they are something of a tourist attraction. Along with flags and painted kerbstones they mark out paramilitary territory.

Electoral politics

The Provisionals had always been wary of involvement in electoral politics. They believed that many nationalists, while supporting the IRA's armed struggle, would prefer to vote for the tried and trusted politicians of the SDLP. A poor vote for declared republicans would undermine the armed struggle. Perhaps more importantly, unless republicans swept the board of nationalist Ireland, they could not claim to speak for Ireland as a whole. The IRA perceived itself as the military expression of the nation's inalienable right to self-determination. Seeking an electoral mandate for its political wing would risk exposing the IRA to the charge of being the armed wing of a minority political party, rather than 'the army of the people'. Thus, in the 1970s, Sinn Féin languished as little more than a social organization for those too timid or too old for 'active service' with the IRA.

It was much by accident, therefore, when Sinn Féin did burst on to the political stage, just when the Provos' military campaign appeared to be approaching irrelevancy. On 5 March 1981 Frank Maguire, Independent MP for Fermanagh/South Tyrone, but quite a traditional republican close to the Provisionals, unexpectedly died. At first unsure how to react, the leadership of Sinn Féin eventually concluded that the opportunity to capitalize on massive Catholic sympathy for the hunger strikers was too good to miss. Bobby Sands was duly nominated. Sands was the hunger striker closest to death. He had joined the IRA after his family had been intimidated by loyalists out of the Belfast estate of

Rathcoole. He had been convicted on a relatively minor charge, arms possession, and whilst in prison wrote poetry and engaging diaries. He was very much the acceptable face of militant republicanism. (In contrast, the Provos' chief strategist in the Maze, Brendan 'Bic' McFarlane, had been convicted for machine-gunning a Protestant pub. This unedifying background resulted in his exclusion from the roster of potential martyrs.)

On 9 April 1981, in a straight contest with Harry West of the Ulster Unionist Party, Sands was elected by 30,492 votes to 29,046. The British government stayed firm despite huge international concern, and on 5 May, after 66 days on hunger strike, Bobby Sands died aged 26. The news was greeted by widespread rioting on a scale not seen since the early 1970s. An estimated 100,000 people attended his funeral in Belfast. In June two hunger strikers (one of whom was to die on strike) were elected to the Dáil in the Republic of Ireland. On 20 August, as the tenth hunger striker succumbed, the last to do so, Owen Carron, who had been Sands's campaign manager, won the Fermanagh/South Tyrone by-election occasioned by Sands's death. At last sure of its potential appeal, Sinn Féin fatefully announced that it would contest all subsequent elections (but would still refuse to take up seats for fear of giving recognition to partitionist institutions). This political turn was buttressed in September when the British Labour Party's annual conference passed a motion committing the party to 'campaign actively' for a united Ireland by consent. Sinn Féin's marked leftward swing, which accompanied its turn to electoral politics, owed something to its desire to appeal to a possible future leftwing Labour government.

On 3 October the hunger strike was called off, as popular fatigue began to set in and continuation increasingly struck observers as suicidal bloodymindedness. The families of hunger strikers still alive made it clear that they would authorize medical intervention to save their sons' lives. Thatcher had not backed down, but the republican movement could claim retrospective victory when, on 6 October 1981, the government announced a series of measures which went a long way to meeting many aspects of the prisoners' five demands. In time POW status was virtually recovered by paramilitary prisoners, facilitating a quasi-amnesty in the 1990s.

In total, ten republican prisoners died on hunger strike; 62 people were killed outside the prison in the accompanying upsurge of violence. Republican violence had not been abandoned, but a new strategy of marrying party politics with 'national resistance' was now to be attempted. At the 1981 Sinn Féin Ard Fheis (annual conference) in Dublin, Danny Morrison justified the new approach: 'Who here really believes we can win the war through the ballot box? But will anyone here object if, with a ballot paper in one hand and the Armalite in the other, we take power in Ireland?'

Sinn Féin's ambition now focused on displacing the SDLP as the primary political expression of nationalism in the north, and building a substantial presence in the south by appealing to the leftist radical inclinations of the working class. Though the movement's rhetoric swung hard to the left, this proved no easy task. SDLP support proved resilient and, when the emotion of the hunger strikes died down, even the alienated youth of the Republic's cities were resistant to being embroiled in the confusing and potentially dangerous politics of 'national liberation'. Attempts to break the logjam struck at the very root of republican theology. Sinn Féin's recognition of the southern state in 1986, allowing its candidates to sit in the Dáil if elected, undermined the movement's claim to be the inheritors of uncompromised national sovereignty. It led, also, to the decamping of the Provisionals' founding members, Sean MacStiofan and Rurai O'Bradaigh. In later taking part in local councils in Northern Ireland, Sinn Féin de facto recognized institutions set up under partition.

Constitutional politics

Sinn Féin's success only confirmed the hostility of the Catholic population to a purely 'internal solution' to the Northern Ireland problem. Having come so tantalizingly close to an institutional recognition of their Irishness in 1974, with Sunningdale's Council of Ireland, they were in no mood to accept Britain's insistence that they settle for anything the Ulster Unionists, now led by veterans of the anti-Sunningdale movement, were likely to offer. Unionism, for its part, saw little need to negotiate seriously. Direct rule was a cheap price to pay for avoiding power sharing and an all-Ireland dimension. Unionists were reasonably satisfied with state pressure on republican violence; loyalist terror had much died down, an indication that popular fears of a military victory for the IRA had receded. Some elements of unionism, including even James Molyneaux, leader of the Ulster Unionist Party, were positively enthusiastic at the idea of direct rule evolving into the full 'integration' of Northern Ireland as an undifferentiated territory of the United Kingdom polity.

The British government was increasingly concerned at this political stasis. As early as May 1980 Thatcher and Charles Haughey, Taoiseach of the Republic, met and jointly commissioned a number of studies on new institutional arrangements, security matters, economic cooperation, and measures to encourage mutual understanding. To this end an Anglo-Irish Intergovernmental Council was established. Thatcher was perhaps primarily concerned to chivvy the Republic into greater security cooperation against the IRA, but Haughey had wider constitutional ambitions. He introduced the phrase 'totality of relationships between these islands' to summarize the dynamic he hoped to see develop.

The southern government was terrified that the northern Catholic population, for which it claimed to act as sponsor, might swing decisively behind Sinn Féin in the aftermath of the hunger strikes. To this end it encouraged the reformulation of constitutional nationalism as an innovative alternative to coercing Ulster Protestants on the one hand, kow-towing to their negotiating veto on the other. Garret FitzGerald's government replaced Haughey's and organized a 'New

Ireland Forum' to discuss ways ahead. This sat from May 1983 to May 1984. The forum was attended by the SDLP from Northern Ireland, and the three main political parties in the Republic: Fianna Fáil (FF), Fine Gael (FG), and the Irish Labour Party. Unionist parties from Northern Ireland were invited but declined to attend. Sinn Féin, wedded to violence, was excluded.

The SDLP had been led by John Hume, a Derry man, since 1979. Gerry Fitt, the previous leader, had resigned because of the party's drift, as he saw it, to traditional nationalism. Hume, however, was a talented strategic thinker. Seeking to redefine nationalism as a pluralistic accommodation, for years he hammered out the phrase 'you can't eat a flag', and his vision of a concept of post-nationalism in Europe became a mainstay. Though repetitious, his persistence did help over time to reconfigure the rhetoric of Irish nationalism. 'Political leadership is like being a teacher', he argued. 'It's about changing the language of others. I say it, and go on saying it until I hear the man in the pub saying my words back to me.'

Under pressure from southern traditionalists, the New Ireland Forum report concluded that 'a united Ireland in the form of a sovereign independent state to be achieved peacefully and by consent' was 'the best and most durable basis for peace and stability'. The symbolic reiteration of traditional objectives dispensed with, it went on to suggest more seriously a federal or confederal state, and joint authority as alternatives. Margaret Thatcher's brusque response shocked and depressed nationalists. Ticking off the forum's proposals she loftily dismissed them one by one: a 'unified Ireland was one solution—that is out. A second solution was a confederation of the two States—that is out. A third solution was joint authority—that is out'. Thatcher's hard-line response can perhaps best be understood in the context of the IRA bombing of the Grand Hotel, Brighton, where her cabinet were staying during the Conservative Party conference. Five people died, several MPs were seriously injured, and Mrs Thatcher was lucky to escape alive. The IRA's statement crowed over this assault on the very basis of British democracy: 'You were lucky this time. But remember, we only have to be lucky once.' Thatcher was not one to be bullied.

The Anglo-Irish Agreement

There was a consensus between the British and Irish governments on the advisability of yet closer governmental cooperation. Early in 1985 the two governments entered into secret negotiations. Thatcher prioritized security, though appreciated that Ulster Catholics might be won from hard-line republicanism by some institutional recognition of the 'Irish dimension'. The southern government was more ambitious, pushing for a form of joint sovereignty over the north to acknowledge the divided loyalties of the province's population and their belief that the historic claim of the island of Ireland on the six counties was at least as great Britain's. Thatcher was unsympathetic to the theory, and dead against the practical implication of diluting unfettered

British sovereignty. But any advance towards the goal of all-Ireland arrangements was better than nothing for nationalists, so the Irish government felt reasonably secure in moderating its demands.

Thus the two governments succeeded in finding common ground, and on 15 November 1985 made public what they had agreed upon. The United Kingdom recognized the Irish Republic's right to be consulted and make proposals concerning Northern Ireland. For its part the Irish Republic reiterated its acknowledgement that a united Ireland could only come about by the consent of the majority of the six-county population. A high-powered Anglo-Irish Intergovernmental Conference was established, to be serviced by a permanent secretariat of civil servants from both jurisdictions, housed at Maryfield in Belfast.

Nationalist Ireland was not at first united on the agreement. Partition hitherto had been rejected as immoral, and accepted only on sufferance as *realpolitik* recognition that Ulster Protestants could by force defy an all-Ireland solution. Nationalists had never acknowledged the right of an arbitrarily defined (as they saw it) 'majority' to opt out of the Irish nation, in much the same way as they had earlier refused the right of an arbitrary majority in the combined islands of Britain and Ireland to hold Ireland in the United Kingdom. It had long been admitted that force against Protestants in the north was not contemplated, but to accept that their majority in the six counties overrode in principle the all-Ireland majority for a united Ireland was a major step. On principle, a southern government would have to reject offers for the 'return' of the north by a British government, or by a devolved government in the north, or by a genuine mass movement centred on nationalist Ulster, but spilling over the border, unless it was specifically approved by the majority of the state of Northern Ireland's population.

The Irish government had already acknowledged the necessity for consent from the majority of Northern Ireland's people in the Sunningdale agreement of 1973. But Sunningdale was only a joint communiqué, while the Anglo-Irish Agreement was an international treaty registered at the United Nations. It is little surprise that many, including Sinn Féin, the party of opposition in the Republic, and even some government ministers and members of the Dáil in the south, were unhappy with the deal.

But nationalist Ireland had indeed gained. There was a definitive recognition by Britain that Dublin had a special responsibility for the north. Garret FitzGerald, the Republic's Taoiseach at the time, described the role of the Irish government as 'less than joint authority, but more than consultation'. Ulster's Catholics enjoyed a new symbolic legitimacy for their national identity. Britain had reiterated, again for the first time in an international treaty, that it would not stand in the way of a united Ireland should consent for this be mustered in Northern Ireland.

Comfort could be found, moreover, in the manner of the agreement's negotiation. If an interim deal did not require Northern Ireland's consent (and the unionist majority of Northern Ireland did emphatically reject the Anglo-Irish Agreement) then further agreements chipping away at the substance of the union between Great Britain and Northern Ireland could be envisaged. Nationalists, even militant republicans, began slowly to contemplate the possibilities for further agreements designed to render the union ever more uncomfortable for Protestants, until they could be brought to agree that an all-Ireland solution might be best. Such a scenario required a British government prepared to ignore unionist protests, but this is precisely what Thatcher's government proceeded to do in the face of a massive protest campaign against the Anglo-Irish Agreement.

15 Margaret Thatcher and Garret Fitzgerald shake hands on signing of Anglo-Irish Agreement, November 1986

Indeed, the Anglo-Irish Agreement was specifically envisaged as a ploy to discomfit unionists. Since Sunningdale they had been unwilling to negotiate constructively because direct rule, even with continuing republican violence, seemed preferable to anything nationalists were likely to accept: power sharing and all-Ireland bodies. Sunningdale had appeared to prove that unionists had a veto not only on the final issue of whether Northern Ireland should be handed over to all-Ireland rule, but even on any interim arrangements unacceptable to them. The Anglo-Irish 'diktat', as they called it, proved them wrong. It explicitly stipulated that only a devolved government within Northern Ireland 'on a basis which would secure widespread acceptance throughout the community . . . achieved . . . with the co-operation of constitutional representatives . . . of both traditions there' could replace the Anglo-Irish Agreement. Unionists were being blackmailed into negotiations. Only a new Sunningdale agreement, i.e. a settlement acceptable to Catholic opinion and thus involving power sharing and a strengthened Irish dimension, could dislodge the Anglo-Irish Agreement. Nationalists, for the first time, had been given a veto of sorts of their own. If this were to work, however, the new dispensation had to withstand unionist fury.

Unionism had fragmented in the late 1960s between those who believed that a majority for the union that included Catholics could be constructed and those who preferred to rely upon ethnic solidarity and the advantages of constitutional incumbency. The collapse of power sharing destroyed the remnants of O'Neillism, outside the APNI. The

Heath government's abolition of the Stormont parliament in 1972 came as a great shock to unionist voters and members of the UUP. The party had ruled the state since its foundation in 1921 and found it difficulty to adjust to the new role of 'opposition' to the government. If devolved government in unionist hands had served as a bulwark against British perfidy or nationalist machinations, the precipice seemed to yawn after its abolition. Unionism was wracked by crisis. The militant Ulster Vanguard movement, led by William Craig, became a separate political party in 1973 and the party split again that year over proposals which led to the Sunningdale agreement. Ian Paisley's DUP, established in 1970, also made considerable inroads into the 'official unionist' vote.

Vanguard, however, fell apart after proposals in 1976 for a voluntary coalition with the SDLP were rubbished in public by Ian Paisley—despite the fact that they were also agreed by his then deputy, William Beattie. More importantly, Ulster's constitutional position calmed in the later 1970s. Britain, after all, seemed unwilling to sell out to the IRA. To back down to terrorism would undermine British authority and leave its liberal democracy open to further blackmail. Loyalist violence indicated that dire unionist warnings of a Protestant backlash were not mere bluff.

This allowed the UUP to consolidate its position as the largest political party in Ulster. But while the party beat off attacks from the DUP, it was at the cost of a conservatism that ruled out all possibility of compromise with moderate nationalism. Although Paisley's DUP finished second to the Ulster Unionists in almost every election, it never polled less than 12 per cent of the overall vote, and on occasion reached 30 per cent. Potential unionist innovation was much restricted by Paisley's formidable presence. Insurgency and direct rule were hardly ideal, but stasis was preferable to innovation, and unionist creativity ossified. The UUP relied upon British determination not to buckle to republican violence. It strategy was little more than one of 'masterful inactivity'.

Passive reliance on British obligations to the province came unstuck with the 1985 Anglo-Irish Agreement. The Ulster Unionist leader, James Molyneaux, warned that Northern Ireland was being delivered 'from one nation to another' and forged an alliance with Ian Paisley's DUP. All Unionist MPs resigned, forcing new elections all over Northern Ireland as a referendum on the agreement. The Unionist vote went up, though they lost the constituency of Newry and Armagh to the SDLP. Unionist-controlled councils boycotted ministers and 'Ulster Says No' banners appeared on local government buildings all over Northern Ireland, including a huge one on Belfast City Hall. Impressive mass demonstrations mobilized the bulk of the province's Protestant population. MPs abstained from normal parliamentary business, a mass petition was sent to Queen Elizabeth, government ministers and boards were boycotted, and local council meetings were suspended. None of this directly impeded the work of the agreement, and the government remained obdurate.

Loyalist violence began to revive, with attacks on Catholics and, an indication of the extent of Protestant alienation, the

RUC. When Margaret Thatcher won the 1987 general election and the Anglo-Irish Agreement was reviewed with no significant changes, however, it was evident the unionist opposition had failed. With the complacent trust in direct rule rudely shattered, argument raged within the Unionist Party on the best way to positively secure Northern Ireland's position. This ranged from equal citizenship, or complete integration with Great Britain, through administrative devolution on the model of the former Greater London Council, to calls for outright Ulster independence. Molyneaux and the leadership generally favoured the 'administrative devolution' option. Although popular within the Young Unionist Movement, the 'equal citizenship' position was greeted coolly within the senior party, as it implied the then 'mainland' British parties—the Tories, Labour, the SDP, and the Liberals—organizing and contesting elections in Northern Ireland against UUP candidates.

There was no immediate rush to negotiations. The agreement, and particularly the secretariat at Maryfield, irked unionists as symbolic of a 'foreign country's' interference in British Ulster. Continuing IRA violence meant that direct rule was not dramatically 'greened' by the agreement. Security remained the priority for Britain, and indeed Thatcher herself grew disillusioned with the agreement as cross-border measures against the IRA were slow to materialize. In the later 1980s the Thatcher government prioritized meeting an IRA offensive. On issues such as security-force killings, obstruction of investigations, collusion, and the composition of the north's courts, Dublin's views and proposals were seen to be rejected repeatedly through the machinery of the agreement.

There was an anxiety, however, that Irish interference worked at an almost molecular level to the advantage of nationalists in Northern Ireland. Unionists were unsettled by the suspicion that Northern Irish society was increasingly being shaped independently of unionism. As much as two thirds of public funds for the regeneration of Belfast went to nationalist areas, as they were most deprived. In mixed North Belfast, scene in the 1970s of strident intimidation, largely from the Protestant side, to enforce demarcation of communities, hundreds of houses in unionist areas by the late 1980s were being razed and replaced by green belts. Protestants tended to move out of the city, as the only area for expansion, the housing estates of West Belfast, were also Catholic and republican strongholds. Though there were sound environmental reasons for this pattern of town planning, suspicious Protestants muttered that the secretariat set up by the Anglo-Irish Agreement was aiming at the 'republicanization' of Belfast.

In fact, this was part of a long-term demographic process, ironically accelerated by the population flights that marked the early years of the Troubles. Working-class Protestants were leaving West and North Belfast and the city side of Derry; rural Protestants moved from the west to the east; middle-class Protestants, particularly those of student age, increasingly left for England and Scotland (net migration to England and Scotland was running at 9,000 per year in the late 1980s). At least half the population now lived in areas which were more than 90 per cent either Protestant or Catholic. As Protestant emigration climbed and Catholics stayed at home, the old ratio of two-thirds Protestant to one-third Catholic gave way to something approaching 45 per cent of the population being Catholic.

Conclusion

From 1972 Britain fixed upon power sharing and a limited all-Ireland dimension as the best resolution of conflicting claims in Northern Ireland. The ability of loyalism to shatter this in the anti-Sunningdale strike of 1974 ensured a continuing high level of Catholic alienation from the state. Briefly Britain flirted with the idea of a radical disengagement, and in doing so delivered renewed hope to the IRA and continuing violence from loyalism. It finally elected from 1976 instead to treat terrorist violence as a criminal rather than political phenomenon. It pursued political negotiations less in hope of resolving the conflict than in keeping Northern Ireland's politicians productively busy.

The IRA fiercely resisted attempts to delegitimize them as a revolutionary army. The hunger strikes emotionally focused this contest of wills with Britain. Its ironic result was to deliver electoral success for Sinn Féin, though it failed to outpace the SDLP. This certainly created difficulties for Britain's policy of 'criminalizing' insurgency. It also undermined the IRA's claim to act on behalf of the Irish nation, however. Rather, the IRA was increasingly recognized as the armed wing of one political party. This could only corrode the theology of armed struggle.

The Anglo-Irish Agreement represented an attempt to engineer real political change. In this it contrasted with sponsorship of fruitless political talks, and indeed the institutions of the agreement were designed to be immune from sabotage by the democracy of Northern Ireland. It marked the Republic's formal acceptance that Irish reunification could not legitimately be imposed on the majority of Northern Ireland. Britain, for its part, admitted that the Republic, as the focus of nationalist aspirations, had the rights of a junior partner in governing Northern Ireland. Unionism was stirred from the comfortable complacency of direct rule in which it had enjoyed a veto on fundamental political change. Slowly an environment for productive negotiation with Northern Ireland emerged.

5

The Long 'Peace'

British policy had developed in the early 1970s as a twin track of levying war and constructing a political dispensation. War, however, delegitimized politics and left the IRA campaign undiminished. With the collapse of the political centre ground, British policy moved to that of limiting conflict to an 'acceptable level of violence' and criminalizing the IRA. This posed serious problems for republicans. Their determination to maintain their self-image as an army led to bitter conflict in the prisons, where their POWs furiously resisted the withdrawal of special category status. The resulting hunger strikes were, by the balance sheet, a remarkable success for republicanism. Not only was de facto political status conceded, but also Sinn Féin was launched into electoral waters on a tidal wave of popular Catholic anger.

Attritional war

Looked at more closely, however, the period introduced new complications into the republican insurgency. The eventual prison regime was liberal but Britain's gift, and prisoners were treated as politicals rather than soldiers. Ironically Sinn Féin's success, and the rather superficial left surge of republican ideology, reinforced this unwelcome transmogrification of republicans from national soldiers to political, indeed party political, revolutionary soldiers.

The young northerners Gerry Adams and Martin McGuinness, hardened in the cauldron of the north and less beholden to abstract republican theology than the southern-based leadership who had established the Provos, had taken over the leadership of the republican movement after the failure of the 1975–6 ceasefire to win any political gains. Indeed, it was widely felt that the open-ended and ill-focused ceasefire had brought the IRA closer to defeat than at any other time during the conflict. It had reorganized and geared towards a long war of attrition, but with a renewed emphasis on developing a non-military political party strategy.

The provisionals' war had entered a grim and dangerous netherworld, however. Whilst 'normalization' brought relief to Catholic communities, republican terrorists were pursued relentlessly. Between 11 November and 12 December 1982 six men were shot dead by the RUC in County Armagh. Five of the dead were members of republican paramilitary organizations, the sixth was a civilian. All six deaths raised suspicions of a police 'shoot-to-kill' policy. The IRA was equally buffeted by 'supergrasses' following the hunger strikes. Borrowing practice from anti-mafia trials, the state offered lavish inducements to informers to secure not merely intelligence, but convictions. By the autumn of 1983 three major super-grass trials had resulted in the conviction of 56, with 31 of these convictions resting solely on the supergrasses' uncorroborated testimony.

Both strategies, in straining the credibility of liberal democratic 'law-and-order' norms, petered out. The shoot-to-kill allegations were subject of a protracted official investigation, and though this was halted in 1988 on the grounds of national security, the deployment of the RUC in lethal ambush operations was obviously abandoned. Similarly, the bulk of the supergrass convictions were overturned by the Court of Appeal on the grounds of unreliability. Military confrontations with the IRA returned to the domain of the army—between December 1983 and February 1985 another ten men were shot dead by SAS undercover squads—while the public face of law enforcement was progressively normalized.

The IRA, buttressed by the importation of substantial quantities (an estimated 30 tons) of weapons and explosive from Libya in 1985–6, attempted to reverse the tide by creating liberated zones in border areas where already troops moved by helicopter rather than by road. Attacks on barracks, which took up considerable IRA resources and resourcefulness, were not without effect, but essentially manoeuvred IRA volunteers in concentrations prone to devastating military counter-strikes. On 8 May 1987, for example, the SAS ambushed an eight-strong IRA active-service unit seeking to destroy the Loughgall RUC station. All IRA men, and an uninvolved civilian, were killed. No liberated areas were possible, and the fruits of political respectability for republicans glistened ever more temptingly.

There was broad acceptance of the leadership's assertion that the movement alone was not strong enough to bring about the conditions necessary to end partition and that allies were needed. After the Anglo-Irish Agreement, a coup for John Hume, Sinn Féin's optimism that it could displace the SDLP declined. Sinn Féin's support by the late 1980s had fallen to 1.2 per cent of the vote in the Irish Republic and 9.2 per cent in Northern Ireland. The SDLP hovered around 20 per cent, and the Irish revolution seemed far off. The republican movement saw its role, now, as stiffening the sinews of a broad nationalist alliance, led by Hume. It still considered armed struggle useful in this regard, as it sustained a political temperature in which moderation, and thus a compromise agreement, would be hard to sustain. The problem was that IRA violence also threatened to exclude the republican movement from the negotiating table. A final settlement might be made over their heads and leave them isolated.

The IRA had always concentrated on sickening British public opinion. And, understanding that British public opinion looked upon the violence in Northern Ireland with horror but relative indifference, they much preferred to kill victims from the British mainland. British army personnel were prioritized, but when the number of military dead surpassed that of British losses in Cyprus, the IRA realized that Britain would or could not easily 'decolonize' Ireland. Direct attacks in Britain raised the profile of the Irish question.

After the Birmingham pub bombings in 1974 the question of Northern Ireland briefly headed the list of political priorities in a British opinion poll (the opprobrium heaped upon the IRA for killing civilians was negative in effect). As locally recruited forces—the RUC and UDR—took the lead in regular patrolling duties from 1976, 'high value' British army targets became correspondingly harder to hit, and 'spectacular' operations on the British mainland became increasingly important in IRA strategy.

In July 1982, for example, the IRA bombed Hyde Park and Regents Park in London, killing two members of the Household Cavalry and six soldiers from the Royal Green Jackets. Politicians were considered 'legitimate targets' and in October 1984 the IRA bombed the Grand Hotel in Brighton during the Conservative Party conference. In 1990 the Conservative MP Ian Gow was assassinated. The aim seemed to be to frighten those politicians prepared to stand prominently by the union.

The 1990s saw a devastating attack on the heart of the British economy. On Friday 10 April 1992 the IRA exploded two bombs at the Baltic Exchange in the centre of London and killed three people including a 15-year-old girl. Insurance claims amounted to £800 million, compared to the estimated figure for the whole of Northern Ireland of £615 million since the start of the Troubles.

Against these bloody but, in IRA terms, successful 'spectaculars' was to be set the increasingly demoralizing attrition in Northern Ireland itself. The bombing of a Remembrance Day service in Enniskillen, on 6 November 1987, in which

eleven Protestant civilians died, was a public-relations dis-
aster, and an embarrassed Gerry Adams pressed the IRA
leadership for greater efforts not to kill 'innocent civilians'.
Even the assassination of 'legitimate targets', however, was
prone to strain the toleration of the broad republican support base. On 6 March 1988 three IRA members were shot
dead in Gibraltar by members of the SAS. A few days later, a
loyalist gunman named Michael Stone killed three mourners
at the funerals of the three. When two British soldiers acci-
dentally drove into the vicinity of the funeral cortège,
another attack was anticipated and they were mobbed and
dragged out of their car. Given fears of a genuine attack, this
was distasteful but perhaps understandable. Less so was their
cold-blooded 'execution' by the IRA, when helpless and
disarmed. This could hardly be defended as 'war'.

The re-escalation of loyalist violence after the Anglo-Irish
Agreement also put the IRA under pressure. Efficient targeting, aided by collusion with individual members of the security forces and perhaps elements of British intelligence, meant
that republican activists were being hit with disturbing regu-
larity in the later 1980s. The exposure of a British agent in
the ranks of the Ulster Defence Association in 1989 simply
unleashed that organization's militants, and the ferocity and
arbitrariness of loyalist attacks on the Catholic community
escalated alarmingly, particularly in North Belfast, South
Derry/East Tyrone, and the Craigavon area extending into
Lisburn. Between 1989 and 1992, 21 Catholics, some republicans, died at the hands of loyalist paramilitaries and the
security forces in the Derry/Tyrone area. The IRA exacted

grim revenge with the murder by landmine of seven Protestant workers at Teebane near Cookstown on 17 January 1992. That they worked for the security forces carried little weight as an excuse with a broad republican community unwilling to see 'their' army disgrace itself. Nor was it even effective, as the Ulster Freedom Fighters murdered five Catholics in a betting shop in Belfast on 5 February 1992 in retaliation.

Efforts to counter loyalist terrorism selectively were no more successful. An attempt in October 1993 to wipe out the leadership of the UFF, meeting in an office over a chip shop on the Shankill Road in Belfast, failed when the bomb went off prematurely. One bomber and nine civilians died. Outrage was universal. Loyalist paramilitaries killed a total of twelve Catholic civilians over the following week. Later that month loyalists shot and killed five, four Catholics and one Protestant, at Greysteel Bar, County Derry. The IRA drew in its horns, for fear of losing its shreds of legitimacy by engaging in internecine sectarian war. Certainly, its inability to stem the tide of loyalist killing was a factor in its eventual decision to 'de-escalate' by calling a ceasefire. In the latter part of 1993 and in the first months of 1994 its violence was directed almost exclusively against the security forces, and incendiary devices replaced car bombs in attacks on 'economic targets'. Loyalists, less choosy in their targets, were killing more than republicans.

The peace process

Despite legion problems with the IRA's armed struggle, there was much suspicion that a renewed ceasefire would impair the movement's unity and élan. The chief fear of republicans was that any protracted cessation would be used by the British government to sap the will and ability of the IRA to wage war—as had been their experience in 1975. Others worried that Sinn Féin would lose its revolutionary edge and become indistinguishable from parties such as Fianna Fáil and the SDLP. Some optimism remained that a combination of low-level war in Northern Ireland—designed to frustrate dialogue and keep lit the beacon of republican resistance—and spectaculars in Britain would chip away at Britain's determination to stand by the unionist people.

Taking note that Britain had faced down unionists over the Anglo-Irish Agreement, and that the SDLP were proving firm in their insistence on an all-Ireland perspective on the problem, the republican movement tentatively considered a 'new departure' in nationalist politics. The Adams-McGuinness leadership hoped that a broad nationalist alliance could be constructed of which the IRA would be an unacknowledged, subordinate, but active part. Just as illegal violence could be disavowed by the broad unionist family, but act as an adjunct nevertheless (in republican thinking), so IRA violence, the Tactical Use of Armed Struggle (TUAS), would evolve into the cutting edge not of Sinn Féin merely, but a broad nationalist alliance including American opinion, the southern Irish government and people, and the SDLP. The IRA had

strengthened its claim to fight for Ireland by adhering to Dáil
Eireann in 1919–21, by espousing Dáil Uladh in the early
1970s, and identifying with the assumed revolutionary
potential of the Irish working class in the late 1970s and
1980s. All these attempts to broaden the republican base had
ultimately failed. Were revolutionary, constitutional, and
émigré nationalism to work informally in harness, an echo of
the Parnellite new departure of the 1870s and 1880s,
renewed political advance might be possible.

Certainly Britain was aware of republican sentiments, and
subtly pressed them on. On 9 November 1991 Secretary of
State Peter Brooke had announced that Britain had no 'self-
ish, strategic, or economic interest in Northern Ireland'
(indeed, Ireland's strategic value to Britain had diminished
with the collapse of the Soviet threat). Behind the scenes the
government held exploratory talks directly with the IRA.

Sensing a change in the wind, John Hume, the leader of
the SDLP, assiduously encouraged the republican movement
along the path of peaceful negotiation, even at the price of
refusing very seriously to engage in negotiations with mainstream unionism. He tentatively entered talks with Gerry
Adams in the late 1980s and again in the early 1990s. On 28
August 1993 they were in a position to issue a joint statement: this rejected an internal settlement and insisted that a
solution must be based 'on the right of the Irish people as a
whole to national self-determination'. This was republican
language, but the qualifier, that 'the exercise of this right
is . . . a matter for agreement between all the people of
Ireland', suggested that the people of Northern Ireland

would have a right to defy a simple all-Ireland numerical majority. This was sailing close to the limits of republican ideology.

The British and Irish governments, in a joint declaration issued from Downing Street on 15 December 1993, agreed 'to foster agreement and reconciliation, leading to a new political framework ... within Northern Ireland, for the whole island, and between these islands', but did not undertake to 'persuade' Protestants to accept Irish unity. This was far short of republican demands, but they were impressed that the governments seemed prepared to respond to the combined weight of Sinn Féin and the SDLP. A secret republican briefing paper considered the political environment in 1994. 'Our goals have not changed', it declared: 'A united 32-county democratic socialist Republic'. However, rather than armed struggle, 'the main strategic objectives to move us towards that goal can be summarised thus. To construct an Irish Nationalist consensus with international support on the basis of the dynamic contained in the Irish peace Initiative.' This was to consist of 'the strongest possible political consensus between the Dublin government, Sinn Féin and the SDLP'. Signalling some degree of principled accommodation, it was admitted that 'an agreed Ireland needs the allegiance of varied traditions to be viable', an obvious echo of John Hume's analysis. It concluded that for 'the first time in 25 years ... all the major Irish nationalist parties are rowing in roughly the same direction'. The novelty of an American administration led by Bill Clinton prepared to act autonomously of the British government on the Northern Ireland question, as when Clinton granted a visa for Adams to visit the US in January 1994, inspired hope that the world's only super-power could be persuaded to act sympathetically to nationalist interests.

On this basis, the IRA called a 'complete and unequivocal' ceasefire on 31 August 1994. Six weeks later, loyalist para-militaries declared a reciprocal ceasefire from 13 October.

The political process

Unionists had some reason to feel anxious at this train of events. Both the UUP and DUP had ended their boycott of the United Kingdom government in September 1987 in order to have talks about the possibility of comprehensive political negotiations. Between 1988 and 1992, there were many attempts to create conditions for all-party talks in Northern Ireland (excluding, because of its support for vio-lence, Sinn Féin). Discussions were to follow three strands simultaneously: relations between the communities within Northern Ireland (strand one), relations between north and south of Ireland (strand two), and relations between the two sovereign governments of the United Kingdom and of the Republic of Ireland (strand three).

The UUP was warming somewhat towards the idea of power sharing and some form of north–south cooperation, if only to regain some control of a situation now dictated, they believed, over their heads by the Anglo-Irish Agreement between the two sovereign governments. It was more than a

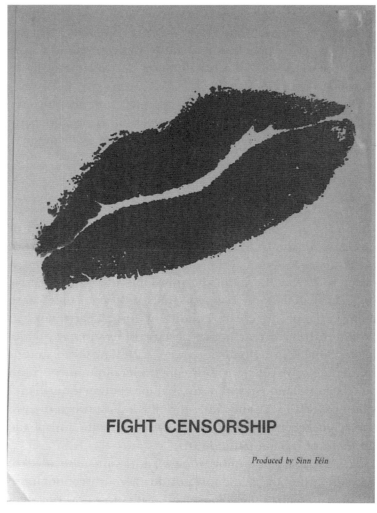

FIGHT CENSORSHIP

Produced by Sinn Féin

16 Sinn Féin 'Fight Censorship' poster. By the 1990s Sinn Féin was downplaying its former militarism to reach out beyond the Catholic ghettos. It was not purely cosmetic

cynical manoeuvre on their part, however. From 1988 onwards, 'responsibility sharing' between nationalist and unionist parties—primarily the UUP and the SDLP—was openly practised by local authorities. By the mid-1990s almost half of the 26 local councils shared responsibility, including some with an infamous reputation for sectarianism.

The SDLP's proposal that Northern Ireland be administered by a six-man Northern Ireland executive commission including one nominee apiece from the British and Irish governments and the European Union smacked too much of joint authority for unionist palates. They concluded that constitutional nationalism was less than sincere about realistic negotiations as long as they were concentrating on bringing republicans in from the cold.

The IRA ceasefire presented a new quandary for unionism. David Trimble of the UUP later conceded that it was the 'event which has caused the greatest problem to unionists in recent years'. Unionists feared that a formidable nationalist alliance, backed up by the threat of renewed IRA violence, was being constructed. Thus they insisted upon an explicitly permanent ceasefire and the 'decommissioning' of terrorist weapons before agreeing to enter into negotiations with Sinn Féin. The Conservative government, led by John Major, recognized unionist fears and pressed the republican movement on these points. In January 1995 Major went further, insisting that joint authority was not on the agenda, that any new arrangements would be negotiated by the parties not imposed by the governments, and that they would be subject to a Northern Ireland referendum. This he offered as 'a triple lock'.

In this delicate balancing act, however, nationalism also had to be placated. In February 1995 two 'framework' documents were issued by the British and Irish governments (one jointly, one by Britain alone). These were rather green in tone and, importantly, future north–south bodies were justified not simply as intergovernmental cooperation, but as recognition of the Irish identity of the north's Catholic minority. Unionists were much put out, and though there was little substantive on the republican agenda on offer, it did something to assuage republican discontent at being kept in the antechamber of negotiations.

A step towards accepting republicans as 'decontaminated' without alienating unionists was the joint communiqué issued from Downing Street in November 1995 proposing a twin-track process, in which talks on decommissioning of paramilitary weapons would take place alongside exploratory talks with all parties including Sinn Féin and loyalist fringe parties associated with Protestant paramilitaries. The aim was for all-party talks to start by the end of February 1996. To reduce the impression that the IRA were being asked to surrender at the behest of Britain and the unionists it was announced that a three-member international body, chaired by former US senator George Mitchell, would advise on arrangements to decommission paramilitary arms. The involvement of America was particularly calculated to appeal to republicans. The president, Bill Clinton, visiting Northern Ireland shortly after the communiqué was released, gave it his imprimatur.

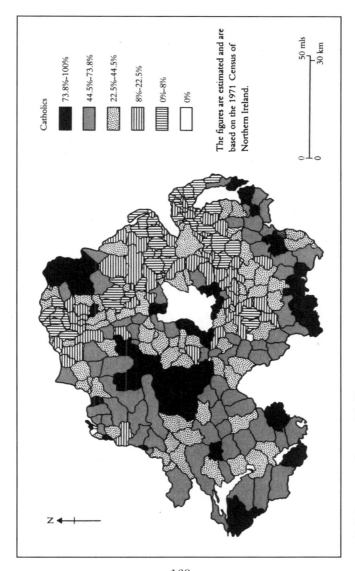

Catholics

73.8%–100%

44.5%–73.8%

22.5%–44.5%

8%–22.5%

0%–8%

0%

The figures are estimated and are based on the 1971 Census of Northern Ireland.

0 ———— 50 mls
0 ———— 30 km

17 Religious spread map of Belfast

On 24 January 1996 the Mitchell Commission published its report. To the discomfiture of the unionists and, indeed, the British government, it argued that paramilitary decommissioning before all-party negotiations was more than could be hoped for. It suggested, instead, that arms be decommissioned in parallel with talks. Mitchell proposed, however, that all parties be required to declare their willingness to pursue purely peaceful means before reaching the negotiating table. Despite unionist outrage, the Major government agreed, but insisted that elections be held for a negotiating convention to reinforce the principle that a democratic mandate, not threat of force, was to be the entry ticket to talks.

Moderate nationalists and the Irish government feared that an election would be seen by republicans as a further delaying tactic, yet another hoop through which to jump. They were right, but IRA hard-liners had long been champing at the bit. TUAS had always suggested the likelihood that, if concessions were considered inadequate, they could be banked and the pressure of 'armed struggle' would be resumed. Even more important was the cardinal priority of keeping the movement united. On 9 February 1996 a huge IRA bomb devastated the Docklands area of London causing damage estimated at £85 million. Two people were killed, more than 100 were injured. The resumption of violence had long been in preparation, and reflected republican anger at apparent 'delaying' tactics by the British government, and, more significantly, a dawning realization that Britain was not preparing to railroad unionists into a dark-green-hued settlement, transitional to a united Ireland. The nature of the bomb—a replication of the Canary Wharf spectacular—and the relatively low-level campaign thereafter (though it did not scruple at murder) indicated, however, that the IRA were not resigned to the end of the peace process and simply resuming war as usual.

All parties and international opinion condemned the campaign roundly and declared their willingness to enter negotiations without waiting for Sinn Féin. Republicans risked a historic marginalization. But when in 29 February 1996 elections were announced, so too was a start-date for negotiations—10 June 1996. A firm deadline was a belated satisfaction of a long-standing republican demand. Still more significantly, after elections to the peace forum, Sinn Féin and other parties need only 'address' the need to decommission terrorist weapons. This was a palpable concession to republicans, but without a renewed ceasefire it would advantage only the loyalist political parties. Political violence remained an absolute barrier to participation.

Elections to the Forum for Peace and Reconciliation were duly held on 30 May 1996. The UUP won 30 seats, the DUP 24 seats, the SDLP 21 seats, the APNI 7 seats, and the United Kingdom Unionist Party (UKUP) 3 seats. Sinn Féin did not suffer from its armed campaign and had its best-ever showing, receiving 17 seats (15.5 per cent of the vote). This, however, expressed the insistence of the republican electorate that it return to non-violence. Four other parties did not win any constituency seats, including the fringe loyalist UDP and PUP, but creative electoral counting squeezed them in as being amongst the top ten most successful parties.

The talks opened on 10 June 1996, with Sinn Féin excluded. Had the IRA wished to sabotage the negotiations, they were presented with a golden opportunity when trouble erupted surrounding loyalist marches in Portadown. A long-standing Twelfth of July Orange Order march returning from a service at Drumcree Church was to be rerouted to avoid the Garvaghy Road, a Catholic area. On this symbolic issue, many loyalists took a stand. When the security services blocked the Orange march, confrontation and rioting ensued. Loyalist protests and roadblocks across the province, in which there was paramilitary involvement, brought much normal activity to a halt. The RUC reversed their decision on 11 June 1996 and allowed the parade to proceed through the Garvaghy Road. Outraged, Catholic areas now erupted into rioting. The forceful reaction of the security forces stood in marked contrast to their incapacity in the face of loyalist intimidation. While 662 plastic bullets were fired at loyalists, thousands were used on nationalists. One youth was killed in Derry, crushed by an armoured car. The IRA, however, stayed its hand. There was to be, Gerry Adams insisted, no violence that wasn't 'consistent with a coherent strategy'. This indicated as nothing else the continuing ascendancy of Adams's and McGuinness's peace strategy within the republican movement.

Progress of talks, however, was barely perceptible. The absence of Sinn Féin, and the pall cast by IRA violence, seemed to stymie any significant advance. No agreement was reached on even the format of negotiations. The election, by landslide, of a United Kingdom Labour government on

1 May 1997, led by Tony Blair, was a rare occasion when a British election benefited political conciliation in Northern Ireland. Unlike Major, Blair was not dependent on Unionist MPs to bolster his shaky majority. He posted as new secretary of state Mo Mowlam, no nationalist indeed, but a touchy-feely free spirit at odds with the preceding succession of colonial-style mandarins. Blair declared the Northern Ireland peace process his highest priority and compart-mentalized 'decommissioning' to a sub-committee. With a new briskness, substantive talks on a political settlement were scheduled to begin in September 1997 and conclude in May the following year. The IRA found this enough to get them off their hook of abstention, and on 20 July 1997 the ceasefire was suddenly restored. After six weeks, Sinn Féin was admitted to the talks.

The DUP immediately walked out, protesting that the IRA had not been required to give up one bullet. The leader of the UUP since 1995, David Trimble, kept his team in. Though elected as something of a hard-liner, Trimble was an imaginative politician. He recognized that, with a rising Catholic population and nationalist vote, together with entrenched involvement from the Irish government and improving coordination between the nationalist parties, Northern Ireland was likely to lose much of its remaining trappings of unequivocally British direct rule. The security services were sure to be reformed and Catholic participation in the state, with all the attendant dangers of a creeping insti-tutionalization of 'Irish' culture, sure to be encouraged. The government's declared commitment to 'parity of esteem'

18 The Good Friday Agreement. Every household in Northern Ireland received a free copy of the agreement with its hopeful cover

threatened to make Northern Ireland a hybrid polity. It seemed best to negotiate a firm political settlement before the unionist position declined further.

Trimble was not merely defensive in vision, however. Whilst his predecessor, James Molyneaux, was temperamentally an integrationist, keen to make Northern Ireland as 'mainland British' as possible, Trimble had long been an enthusiastic advocate of devolution. Indeed, he had flirted with ideas of dominion status and even Ulster independence. This reflected a genuine belief in the cultural distinctiveness of Ulster culture, born of a confluence of traditions. He envisaged a form of Ulster citizenship, within an increasingly pluralistic United Kingdom, that would reach out to at least a section of Catholics. Even links with the Republic of Ireland, if in the context of an emerging political alliance of the British Isles, would be a boon, not a burden.

The Belfast Good Friday Agreement

Republicans had certainly won tactical victories in gaining entry to the talks for Sinn Féin without decommissioning, never mind the dismantling of its paramilitary forces. Indeed, it was kept on a war footing. Briefly, in early 1998, Sinn Féin was excluded from the talks as a nominal punishment for IRA involvement in the killing of a loyalist paramilitary and a Catholic drugs dealer. Many other activities, most especially brutal 'punishment beatings', went almost unremarked. Loyalist violations of their ceasefire equally attracted only minor sanctions. When it came to the substantive negotiations, however, Sinn Féin found itself with little influence. These were dominated by Trimble's UUP and Hume's SDLP.

In practice, the SDLP presented proposals designed to maximize the all-Ireland dimension and Dublin involvement as acknowledgement of and guarantor for the Catholic minority's Irish identity. In a break from previous positions, however, they did not strive for a dynamic that would progressively integrate the island at the cost of British influence. The Ulster Unionists, recognizing this, were content largely to react, striving to moderate the all-Ireland dimension and fixing it as the final dispensation.

The two governments were well content with this situation. Their ambition had always been to wean republicanism away from violence. Any cost in terms of ultimate republican objectives—i.e. the installation of a mechanism progressively to undermine the union with Britain—had to be minimized for fear of alienating the unionists. Thus, when in January 1998 the governments produced a 'heads of agreement' document, outlining areas of agreement and disagreement and likely resolutions, they took as their lead the negotiating positions of the Ulster Unionists and the SDLP. Not surprisingly, Sinn Féin were irked; they rejected the document but were helpless to do much else.

Senator George Mitchell, as the talks faltered, took the unexpected step of moving the final date forward. This concentrated minds. British Prime Minister Tony Blair and Irish Taoiseach Bertie Ahern weighed in to apply diplomatic pressure. Last-minute haggling focused on police reform, decommissioning, and the early release of paramilitary prisoners. David Trimble found it impossible to bring his entire negotiating team through to the finish—his deputy, Jeffrey Donaldson, walking out. Nevertheless, agreement was eventually reached some seventeen hours after the deadline, at around 5 p.m. on Good Friday, 10 April, 1998.

The Belfast, or Good Friday, Agreement, was multi-faceted and balancing. Internally, a power-sharing arrangement gave representatives of each community a veto over the other. Legislation in the devolved assembly required either parallel consent or a weighted majority of 60 per cent of voting members to be passed. Sub-committees would oversee executive functions, their membership being in broad proportion to party strengths in the assembly and the chairs allocated proportionately. Each department was to be headed by a minister with full executive authority. Ministers, thus, were not required to agree with each other in a cabinet, the norm in a representative democracy. All main parties would be given their personal fiefdom, subject only to the assembly. A civic-forum 'talking shop' was to cater for fringe political elements excluded from the assembly for lack of democratic mandate, and to foster political consensus on social and economic issues present in civil society if not in the polarized party structure.

The British secretary of state was to remain responsible for non-devolved matters—significantly, law and order—and to represent Northern Ireland in the United Kingdom. There was to be a north–south ministerial council. A further agreement gave the north–south bodies competence to discuss matters covering transport, agriculture, education, health, environment research, and tourism. Delegations to the north–south bodies would be responsible to the Northern Ireland Assembly and the Dáil respectively.

Sinn Féin had no hand in negotiating these institutions. They were primarily the work of the UUP and the SDLP. Sinn Féin had presented a traditional republican analysis, predicting ordered absorption of Protestants into an independent united Ireland if Britain cut them adrift. Its real aim had been to green the culture of Northern Ireland. With this it had some success. Paramilitary prisoners associated with paramilitary groups on ceasefire would be released within two years and a commission would propose police reform. There were commitments to enhance the status of the Irish language and to reinforce existing measures aimed at guaranteeing fair employment and an end to discrimination. These were not simply for nationalists. Loyalists would be released and Ulster-Scots, a dialect hastily promoted to the status of full-scale language, would benefit in proportion to the Irish language.

The overall impact, however, would be disproportionately to legitimize militant Irish culture. Loyalist prisoners were fewer and more importantly enjoyed rather less pretension as national soldiers. Any infusion of Gaelic culture would dilute Ulster's Britishness, Ulster-Scots being too inchoate a phenomenon to counter-balance. 'Parity of esteem' ruled out the institutional domination of British and Protestant culture.

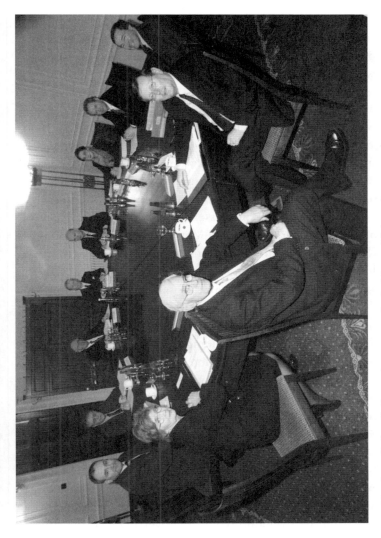

19 Northern Ireland's Executive pose at the 'cabinet table', 2000

Unionists made significant gains in fortifying the union, even if this meant retreating from advanced positions. They had a devolved Northern Ireland government enjoying veto power over the north–south bodies. The Irish government committed itself to amending its constitution in order to withdraw the territorial claim on the north. The 1985 Anglo-Irish Agreement would be replaced by a new British–Irish Agreement, though it was unlikely that the British–Irish axis established by the agreement would much change. As a speculative counter to the cultural shift towards 'Irishness' threatened by the agreement, unionists won a British–Irish Council (involving the new assemblies for Northern Ireland, Scotland and Wales, the Isle of Man and the Channel Islands, and the British and Irish parliaments). This accorded with a belief that a pluralistic British Isles would progressively diminish Irish nationalist separatism. Once more, the principle of no constitutional change without the consent of the majority in Northern Ireland was reiterated as an absolute.

The DUP rejected the agreement; the UUP, if not without dissension, stood by their leader. The SDLP were delighted, but Sinn Féin saw it as only creating terrain for a new, though probably non-military, struggle. On these grounds they counselled a yes vote in the subsequent referenda on both sides of the border. The agreement was endorsed in Northern Ireland by 71.1 per cent of voters, in the Republic by 95 per cent. Controversially, however, British Prime Minister Tony Blair was forced to bolster the pro-agreement unionist position by promising that those who used or threatened violence would be excluded from the government of Northern

Ireland. Thus the clock was reset on the timer for IRA decommissioning. Even then, nearly half of unionist voters opposed the deal.

In the subsequent elections to the assembly some 75.5 per cent of votes cast were for candidates in favour of the agreement. Eighty seats were won by parties in favour and 28 by those against. However, the UUP had been unable to maintain a united front. Its 21 per cent of the vote put it in second position to the SDLP on 22 per cent, though it was ahead on seats, thus allowing David Trimble to become first minister of the new devolved executive. For the first time unionists were no longer the largest single party by votes. Legislation to give effect to the Belfast Agreement became law in June 1998. Unionists, however, were deeply unhappy with the early release of prisoners and horrified at the 'rebranding' scheme proposed for the RUC—in order to raise Catholic participation from a dismal 7.5 per cent of total personnel, and nationalist participation from close to zero—to become the Northern Ireland Police Service. Determined not to appear the defeated 'army', the IRA refused to placate unionist fears by decommissioning weapons.

Part of the success of the peace process was based upon deliberate ambiguity. The British and Irish governments, assuming the tenacity of communal polarization, saw it as a segregatory but cooperative and balanced settlement. Both harboured some hope of eventual amelioration of division, and the Irish government at least hoped for some form of united Ireland. Republicans, and to a lesser extent the

---

Identities

Two-thirds of Protestants, but only one-tenth of Catholics, describe themselves as 'British'; by contrast, three in five Catholics, but only one in fifty Protestants, describe themselves as 'Irish'.

There exists a substantial level of Catholic support for a settlement within Northern Ireland, with certain conditions attached. In 1972, at the height of nationalist insurrection, 41 per cent of Catholics said that they would vote against the unification of Ireland, and 6 per cent that they would abstain. Peace appears to have strengthened Catholic belief in the utility of a united independent Ireland. Support amongst Catholics stood at 55 per cent in June 1998 at the time of the Good Friday Agreement. It rose to 59 per cent by 2001. Overall support for a united Ireland went up from 25 per cent to 27 per cent, while the level of support for the retention of the union fell over the same period from 63 per cent to 58 per cent. However, only 2 per cent of Protestants were prepared to back a united Ireland.

Unionists have some hope of maintaining the union even if, as is possible, Catholics become a numerical majority within 20 years or so. Assuming 70 per cent of Catholics supported Irish unity (and that no Protestants did) a majority in favour of unification would require that the adult Catholic population be more than two and a half times larger than the Protestant population.

Despite Catholic moderation on the constitutional question, their politics is shaped by their sense of identity, not their sense of the possible. Just under 90 per cent support

---

nationalist parties. Protestants, defending a status quo, are just as firm despite a somewhat hazier sense of identity. Just under 90 per cent support unionist parties.

Some 28 per cent of Catholics sympathize with republican paramilitaries as 'soldiers of the nation'. 31 per cent of Protestants sympathize with loyalist paramilitaries as the ultimate weapon of retaliation and defence of the union.

SDLP and Catholics as a whole, placed a greater burden of expectation on such amelioration, or at any rate insidious undermining of Protestant faith in the advantages of an unenthusiastic and compromised union. Many Protestants, aware of such agendas, rejected the settlement, but a substantial body saw much to be played for in the prolonged and open-ended period of anticipated evolution. They hoped and believed that bedding down would permit the emergence of a pro-union minority amongst Catholics that would underpin the union indefinitely.

Most unionists hoped that the Northern Ireland Assembly would eclipse the north–south bodies and British–Irish axis. Nationalists, by contrast, intended to involve as many actors as possible, maintaining London, Dublin, and Washington as important participants. Thus unionists focused on the devolved administration, with party leader Trimble at its head and even the DUP participating in the executive. On the nationalist side, however, the SDLP leader, John Hume, left the assembly altogether to concentrate on the international arena, while Gerry Adams decided against taking office in the devolved executive.

Loyalist unhappiness with the agreement grew steadily, but the prospect of released prisoners facing reincarceration acted as a restraint upon a full resumption of violence. A steady stream of low-level sectarian attacks—the continuing pattern of displacing Catholics from Protestant zones—indicated the potential for a greater outbreak. Loyalist assassinations, sometimes drug related, sometimes political, continued. The IRA suffered splintering, with the continuing campaign conducted by the Continuity IRA and the 'Real' IRA. The latter pursued a succession of car-bomb attacks on town centres. On 15 August 1998, following a misleading warning, an explosion in Omagh killed 29, the largest single atrocity of the Troubles. Such horror, ironically, reinforced a fundamental change in the popular mindset: murderous violence for political ends had returned to the realms of the unacceptable. As Bloody Sunday unleashed the demons, Omagh reined them in. The 'unarmed struggle' was developing a momentum of its own. Faced with a threat from Trimble to collapse the agreement if progress was not made on IRA decommissioning, and calculating that republicans would lose out in the subsequent 'blame game', the IRA pledged in May 2000 to put its weaponry 'beyond use' at some unspecified time and in the meantime open some of its weapons dumps to international monitors.

For the IRA leadership, however, TUAS remained as at least a theoretical possibility (less theoretical, if one considered Provo violence directed against political and social dissidents within their 'own' communities). On 25 February, the secretive IRA leader Brian Keenan told an audience of the faithful, 'Don't be afraid of the phase we are in. This phase will either be successful, or it will be over. The Good Friday agreement will either stand, or it will fall.' He insisted the peace pact's collapse wouldn't stop Irish republicans from achieving 'liberty and equality. . . . Until we get that, we'll use each and every phase of struggle to prosecute the revolution towards those ends.'

Trimble, in his own way, recognized that peaceful politics was 'war by other means', as he told his party conference in October 2000. In November 2000, as first minister (though possibly beyond his powers), he banned Sinn Féin ministers from participating in the north–south bodies in a bid to force progress on IRA decommissioning. It only succeeded in souring the atmosphere. Trimble announced that he would resign on 1 July 2001 as first minister in the absence of actual IRA decommissioning. Nevertheless, he was badly mauled in the subsequent United Kingdom general election. His Ulster Unionist Party lost about a sixth of their support, while the DUP increased theirs by more than 50 per cent. Sinn Féin for the first time outstripped the SDLP, improving its vote by about a third, while the SDLP fell by about an eighth. The minor parties were squeezed, and the big four finely balanced (UUP—26.8 per cent, DUP—22.5 per cent, SF—21.7 per cent, SDLP—21.0 per cent). Seven of the eighteen Northern Ireland seats changed hands, the west going notably green and Sinn Féin doubling its complement from two to four. The SDLP lost one, the DUP went from two to five, while the UUP lost net four, from ten to six. Clearly, the new dispensation, rather than soften division, increased nationalist optimism, even triumphalism, at the expense of growing unionist suspicion and truculence.

Trimble's resignation went ahead and a new round of negotiations began. Both governments worked to present enough on police reform and ancillary issues to induce substantial IRA decommissioning. Meanwhile vicious sectarian riots reminiscent of 1969 scarred interfaces in Belfast during the summer of 2001 and a disillusioned loyalism began to unwind its ceasefire.

With paramilitarism intact, and unionists deeply suspicious of the direction the Good Friday Agreement threatened to take them, dark clouds remained stark against the blue skies.

Conclusion

Largely through the efforts of the British government, but also helped by intellectual revisionism, demographic changes, rising prosperity, the entry of republicanism into electoral politics and the end of the Cold War, the language of the Northern Ireland conflict slowly mutated. The overt unionist insistence upon the absolute rights of the majority, and the militarism of paramilitary nationalism were increasingly displaced by rhetoric of inclusiveness and peacemaking. The change in discourse marked not an end to polarization between Catholic and Protestant, but it did facilitate a shift from mutually uncomprehending stalemate.

Unionism negotiated peace because it saw that only through arriving at a definitive settlement could it halt the erosion of unionism's position. It faced a rising Catholic population and a politically powerful nationalist bloc that now had formal recourse to the government of the Republic when making representations. The Irish Republic was enjoying precocious economic success, and was ostentatiously modernizing by repudiating much of its traditional Roman Catholic piety. This threateningly raised the credibility of the nationalist critique of partition, but also seemed to render it sufficiently materialist to be amenable to negotiation. Many unionists feared, however, that a settlement would not shield the union from further assault, but merely ratchet the politics of the province further towards the nationalist agenda. Paisley's DUP benefited from this disillusionment.

The SDLP were prepared seriously to treat the Good Friday Agreement as a 'final settlement', but their espousal of post-nationalist politics denied the reality that the Catholic electorate hoped for further gains. Sinn Féin seemed poised to definitively outstrip their rivals. Their ambitions were much reduced, however. The theology that the IRA had the moral right to impose the 30-county republic on all minorities, including the majority in Northern Ireland, was a dead letter. Republican strategy now seemed to concentrate upon facilitating Irish reunification in the event of a Catholic majority in the province, to this end maintaining nationalist enthusiasm and undermining the unionist will to resist.

Many commentators in the summer of 2001 thought the gulf between the two communities—in their aspirations and social lives—to have been wider than at any time in the previous 30 years.

Rhetoric remains divisive. Unionists see nationalists as slippery and disingenuous, nationalists are distressed at their perception of a unionist lack of imagination and unwillingness to engage creatively. But when it has operated, a wide-based devolved government in Northern Ireland has been surprisingly successful.

6

Conclusion

Who won and who lost? Certainly, unionists cannot hope to return to an Ulster of old, securely British in all manifestations of state culture. The Troubles have locked Northern Ireland irreversibly into an Irish paradigm. Institutional recognition of this, in all-Ireland bodies, is likely to be permanent. Nor can nationalists have faith that Ireland will become 'Gaelic and free', shunning its community with Great Britain. The principle that only Northern Ireland can consent to fundamental constitutional change is more firmly enshrined now than when the violence began.

That violence was almost completely pointless seems clear, but it is likely that reference to war will colour and shape politics for long to come. This memory may infect a new generation with ready-made traditions of war, but equally old soldiers can drive their energies, with more effect, into peaceful politics. The echo of bombs and bullets must remain preferable to their bloody immediacy.

The potential exists now in Northern Ireland for an experiment important in the wider world. Can two identities and national allegiances be accommodated in the same state without oppression, rebellion, or violence? That divergent identities exist can hardly be doubted, but the test is whether these can be institutionally recognized to the satisfaction of both. Further, if Northern Ireland is to escape the debilitating tension of continuous communal competition, space must be allowed for the development of a politics and society no longer polarized between Protestant and Catholic.

This is no easy task, and the evidence suggests that politicians at least see a continuing need to rally and manoeuvre in a never-ending struggle to preserve and favour their respective traditions. In a developing climate of peace and cooperation, however, it may be hoped that for most citizens of Northern Ireland the clash of ideology, while not irrelevant to their lives, will become a background hum to each individual's day-to-day life. A sense of identity can liberate as well as bind; strong allegiances can provide secure jumping points for the investigation of other cultures, histories, and ways of life. It is to be hoped that Northern Ireland will grow not only in prosperity, but also in self-confidence. In the future, though not for some time, it may yet become a beacon for culture and pluralism.

References

For many of the quotes and much of the information in this book, I have drawn upon:

Don Anderson, *Fourteen May Days: The Inside Story of the Loyalist Strike of 1974* (Dublin: Gill and Macmillan, 1994).

Paul Arthur, *The People's Democracy 1968–1973* (Belfast: Blackstaff Press, 1974).

Ciarán de Baróid, *Ballymurphy and the Irish War* (Dublin: Aisling Publishers, 1989).

Patrick Bishop and Eamonn Mallie, *The Provisional IRA* (London: Corgi Books, 1988).

Brian Campbell, *Nor Meekly Serve my Time: The H Block Struggle 1976–1981* (Belfast: Beyond the Pale, 1998).

Charles Carlton, *Bigotry and Blood: Documents on the Ulster Troubles* (Chicago: Nelson Hall, 1977).

Sean Cronin, *Irish Nationalism: A History of its Roots and Ideology* (London: Pluto Press, 1980).

Paddy Devlin, *Straight Left: An Autobiograhy* (Belfast: Blackstaff, 1993).

Paddy Doherty and Peter Hegarty, *Paddy Bogside* (Dublin: Mercier Press, 2001).

Michael Farrell, *Northern Ireland: The Orange State* (London: Pluto, 1983).

Roy Garland, *The Ulster Volunteer Force: Negotiating History* (Belfast: Shankill Community Publication, 1991).

Desmond Hamill, *Pig in the Middle: The Army in Northern Ireland 1969–1985* (London: Methuen, 1985).

A. C. Hepburn, *The Conflict of Nationality in Modern Ireland* (London: Edward Arnold, 1980).

Maria Maguire, *To Take Arms: A Year in the Provisional IRA* (London: Quartet Books, 1973).

Sean MacStiofain, *Revolutionary in Ireland* (Edinburgh: Gordon Cremonesi, 1975).

Eamonn McCann, *War and Peace in Ireland* (Dublin: Hot Press Books, 1998).

Marc Mulholland, *Northern Ireland at the Crossroads: Ulster Unionism in the O'Neill Years* (Basingstoke: Macmillan, 2000).

Sarah Nelson, *Ulster's Uncertain Defenders: Protestant Political, Paramilitary and Community Groups and the Northern Ireland Conflict* (Belfast: Appletree Press, 1984).

Brendan O'Brien, *The Long War: The IRA and Sinn Féin* (Dublin: The O'Brien Press, 1999).

Conor Cruise O'Brien, *States of Ireland* (London: Hutchinson, 1972).

Sean O'Callaghan, *The Informer* (London: Corgi, 1999).

Conor O'Cleary, *Phrases Make History Here: A Century of Irish Political Quotations* (Dublin: The O'Brien Press, 1986).

Alan O'Day and John Stevenson (eds.), *Irish Historical Documents since 1800* (Dublin: Gill and Macmillan 1992).

Mitchell O Snodaigh, *Irish Political Documents, 1916–1949* (Dublin: Irish Academic Press).

Paul Routledge, *John Hume: A Biography* (London: Harper Collins, 1998).

Rosita Sweetman, *On Our Knees: Ireland 1972* (London: Pan Books, 1972).

Peter Taylor, *Provos: The IRA and Sinn Fein* (London: Bloomsbury, 1997).

Further Reading

There are far too many good books on Northern Ireland to mention here. There are two excellent surveys of literature on Northern Ireland: John Whyte's *Interpreting Northern Ireland* (Oxford: OUP, 1990) is judicious and humane, John McGarry and Brendan O'Leary's *Explaining Northern Ireland* (Oxford: Blackwells, 1995) acerbic and witty.

Good historical accounts are R. F. Foster's *Modern Ireland* (London: Allen Lane, 1988), a perceptive and original classic, and *Alvin Jackson's Ireland 1798–1998* (Oxford: Blackwells, 1999) is a great, primarily political account. Very well worth reading is A. T. Q. Stewart's *The Narrow Ground: The Roots of Conflict in Ulster* (London: Faber and Faber, 1977, 1989).

For the Stormont era see Patrick Buckland, *The Factory of Grievances* (Dublin: Gill and Macmillan, 1975), Eamon Phoenix, *Northern Nationalism* (Belfast: Ulster Historical Foundation, 1994), and Paul Bew, Peter Gibbon, and Henry Patterson, *The State in Northern Ireland* (London: Serif, 1996).

The history of the Unionist Party is covered by John F. Harbinson, *The Ulster Unionist Party 1882–1973* (Belfast: Blackstaff, 1973) and David Hume, *The Ulster Unionist Party 1972–92* (Lurgan: Ulster Society, 1996).

For moderate nationalism see Ian McAllister, *The Northern Ireland Social Democratic and Labour Party* (London: Macmillan, 1977) and biographies of John Hume by Barry White (Belfast: Blackstaff, 1984) and Paul Routledge (London: HarperCollins, 1998).

There are many books on the IRA. Good accounts include M. L. R. Smith, *Fighting for Ireland?* (London: Routledge, 1995), a military analysis, and Henry Patterson, *The Politics of Illusion* (London: Lawrence and Wishart, 1997), a political analysis.

The best book on loyalism is Steven Bruce, *The Red Hand* (Oxford: OUP, 1992).

Crucial theoretical analyses are Richard Rose, *Governing Without Consensus* (London: Faber and Faber, 1971), based upon a survey of political opinions concluded just prior to the outbreak of the Troubles, and Frank Wright, *Northern Ireland: A Comparative Perspective* (Dublin: Gill and Macmillan, 1987), challenging but rewarding.

The CAIN Website, at http://cain.ulst.ac.uk/, contains a huge amount of excellent material on the Web, including many official documents and book extracts. Very good maps can be found on The Ireland Story site, http://www.irelandstory.com/. For a daily digest of newspaper articles on Northern Ireland, see Newshound, http://www.nuzhound.com/.

Index

abstention policy 58, 78. 116, 150, 173
Adams, Gerry 105, 156, 163, 165, 172, 183
Ahern, Bertie 176
Alliance Party, see APNI (Alliance Party of Northern Ireland)
American Civil War 86
Andrews, J. M. 57
Anglo-Irish Agreement (1985) 144–53, 180
Anglo-Irish Intergovernmental Conference (1985) 145
Anglo-Irish Intergovernmental Council (1981) 131, 142
Anglo-Irish Treaty (1921) 83, 85
anti-home rule 20, 51
Antrim, County 1, 2, 9, 28, 42
APNI (Alliance Party of Northern Ireland) 117, 148, 171
Apprentice Boys parades 71
Ardoyne 72
Ards peninsula 3
Armagh, city of 69
Armagh, County 2
  casualties 93
  partition 28
  riots (1969) 72
  SAS 127
  sectarian balance 8, 15
  stability of Unionist vote 42, 46
  violence in 10

Armagh District Council 47
arms searches 91–2
arms supplies 157
arrest procedures 32
Asquith, Herbert Henry 24, 25
assassinations 107, 129, 159, 160

B-Specials (police auxiliaries) 62, 65, 71, 76
Ballymurphy estate, Belfast 101
Baltic Exchange bombing 159
barricades 73, 79, 96, 99, 172
Bates, Dawson 54
Beattie, William 149
Belfast
  bombs in 69, 106
  British army 72, 73, 87, 90, 91–2, 97–8
  industrial growth in 14–15
  population displacement 76
  regeneration funds for 152
  rioting 13–14, 16, 17, 70, 72–3
  sectarian balance in 15
  in 1790s 8
  student march 69
  Unionist vote in 42, 44–5
  victims of violence 93
  violence during 1922 31
Belfast Agreement, see Good Friday Agreement
Bennet Report (1979) 127
Birmingham pub bombings 159

Birmingham Six 123
Blair, Tony 173, 176, 180
Bloody Sunday (1971) 97
Bogside, Londonderry 71–2, 106
Bombay Street, see Falls Road area
bombing campaigns
    IRA 94, 98, 106, 128, 161
    loyalist 67–8
    mainland 123, 144, 159, 170
    republican splinter groups 184
Boundary Commission 34
British army 74–7, 129
    in Belfast 72, 73, 87, 90, 91–2
    Bloody Sunday 97–8
    casualties 93, 94–5
    counter-insurgency operations
        122, 127, 157
    Hyde/Regents Park bombings
        159
    intelligence report on IRA 89
    IRA 79, 97–101
    Operation Motorman 106
    SAS undercover squads 127,
        157, 160
    Ulster Defence Regiment 110
British-Irish Agreement 180
Brooke, Basil (later Lord
    Brookeborough) 29, 49
Brooke, John 108
Brooke, Peter 163
Bunting, Roy 68
Burntollet Bridge (1969) 64, 69
Butt, Isaac 18

Cahill, Joe 95
Callagan, Jim 108
Canary Wharf 171

car bombs 106, 184
Carron, Owen 139
Carson, Edward (later Baron
    Carson) 21, 23, 25, 30, 39
Casement, Roger 85
Castlereagh holding centre 32
Catholics 34–5, 88
    attitude to IRA 115
    attitude to security forces 98
    Belfast workforce 15
    birth rate 30, 51, 60
    British army and 74, 89–90
    curfews 91–2
    economic discrimination 46,
        48–54
    following partition 31
    home rule 17–25, 19–20
    identity 182–3
    liberal-nationalist alliance
        26–7
    martial pride 101–2, 130–1
    O'Neillite project 59–60, 65,
        66
    penal legislation against 6
    plantation policy 3
    population displacement 76
    proposed five-point reforms
        63–4
    rioting in August 1969 71–4
    1641 rebellion 3–4
    at Stormont 58, 78
Cavan 2
ceasefire proposals 102, 104
ceasefires 105, 109, 124, 161,
    165
censuses 47
Chamberlain, Neville 40

Charles I, King 3
Chichester-Clark, James 70, 95
Church of Ireland 17–18
Churchill, Winston 25
civil rights 21, 54, 60, 61, 62–4,
    65, 66, 67–9, 112
civil service 57, 59
civil war (1922–3) 84
Cleary, Peter 127
Clinton, Bill 164–5, 168
Clonard area, Belfast 72
Cold War 163
Coleraine 1
collusion 110, 125
Communism 85
Community Relations
    Commission 76
complaints procedures 32
Connacht 9
conscription 28
Conservative government 140,
    144, 149, 167–8, 170, see also
    individual prime ministers
Conservative Party 131
    Grand Hotel bombing 144, 159
consumer spending 52
Continuity IRA 184
Conway, Cardinal 60–1
Conway Street area, Belfast 72
Cookstown massacre (1992) 161
Copcutt, Geoffrey 53
Corrigan, Mairead 129
cottage industries 14, 15
cotton industry 14
Council of Ireland 117–18, 119,
    121, 141
Courtaulds 51

Craig, Bill 44, 64, 68, 106–7, 118,
    149
Craig, James (later Lord
    Craigavon) 29, 34, 44, 53,
    54
Craigavon (city) 53
Craigavon meeting (1911) 23
Cromwell, Oliver 4
Crumlin Road, Belfast 72, 73
CS (tear) gas 33, 71, 91, 99
culture 11–12, 27, 178
curfews 91–2
Curtis, Gunner Robert 94
Cyprus 158

Dáil Éireann 28, 81–2, 84, 85,
    102, 103, 141, 146, 163
Dáil Uladh 102, 103, 163
Davitt, Michael 19
de Valera, Éamon 40, 49, 85
decommissioning 167, 168, 170,
    171, 173, 181, 184, 185, 186
Derry city, see Londonderry, city
    of
Devlin, Bernadette 70
Devlin, Joe 34–5
Devlin, Paddy 91
devolution 47, 116, 131, 148–9,
    175, 177–86
Devoy, John 19
Diplock (non-jury) courts 32,
    127
direct rule 104–5, 113, 121,
    131, 132, 141, 148
discrimination 61
    electoral 45–8
    employment 49–50, 55–8

disestablishment 17–18, 20
Dobson, John 47–8
Docklands bomb (1996) 170
Dolly's Brae (1849) 10, 12
Donaldson, Geoffrey 177
Donegal 2
Down, County 1, 2, 28, 42
Downing Street Declaration
    (1969) 113
Downing Street Declaration
    (1993) 164
Drew, Thomas 17
Drogheda massacre (1649) 4
Drumcree marches 98–9, 172
Du Pont 50, 52
Dublin 25, 28, 30, 34, 77
Dublin Metropolitan Police 83
Dundalk 70
Dungannon 14
DUP (Democratic Unionist
    Party) 118, 149–50, 165,
    171, 180, 181

Easter Rising (1916) 27, 81, 85
economic discrimination 48–55
economy 51–3
Edenderry Inn, north Belfast
    70
education 12, 49, 52
elections
    Forum for Peace and
        Reconciliation 171
    general (1997) 172–3
    general (2001) 185
    Northern Ireland Assembly
        181
electoral discrimination 45–8

Elliott, George 50
emergency powers legislation
    32–3, 62, 122
employment discrimination
    49–50, 55–8
EMU (Education for Mutual
    Understanding) 12
English Civil War 4
Enkelon 51
Enlightenment 7
Enniskillen 44
    bombing in 1987 159–60
Enniskillen Housing Trust 50
EPA (Emergency Powers Act) (1973)
    32
equal citizenship 151
European Union 53, 167

Falls Road area, Belfast 72, 73, 79
famine 2, 10
Farrel, Mairéad 134
Faulkner, Brian 95, 105, 117,
    118, 120–1
Fenianism 85
Fermanagh, County 2
    local government boundaries
        47
    partition 28
    stability of Unionist vote 44
Fianna Fáil (FF) 143, 162
Fine Gael (FG) 143
firefights 99, 101, 129
First World War 25–8, 80
Fitt, Gerry 114, 143
Fitzgerald, Garret 142–3, 146,
    147
forced confessions 127

Forestry Commission 59
Forum for Peace and
     Reconciliation 171
fraternization 92
Free State 83–4
French Resistance 80
French Revolution 7, 9
Friel, Brian 11
funeral attacks 160

Garvagh, battle of (1813) 10
Gaulle, Charles de 80
general strike (1974) 119–21
George III, King 8
gerrymandering 47, 48, 53–4,
     54–5, 59
Gervaghy Road, Portadown 172
Gibraltar 160
Gladstone, William Ewart 17, 19,
     20
Glorious Revolution 4, 8
Good Friday Agreement (1998)
     33, 94, 174, 176–87
Goulding, Cathal 78
Government of Ireland Act
     (1920) 28–9, 103
Gow, Ian 159
Grand Hotel, Brighton 144, 159
Great Famine (1845–50) 10
Great War, see First World War
Green Book 85
Greysteel Bar massacre 161
guerrilla conflict 82–3
Guildford Four 123

Harland & Wolff shipyard, Belfast
     51

Harris, Rosemary 11
Hastings, Max 73–4
Haughey, Charles 142
health provision 52
Heaney, Seamus 11–12
Hearts of Down 9
Heath, Edward 79, 149
Henry VIII, King 2
Hierome, Mr (Minister) 4
holding centres 32
Home Government Association
     18
home rule 17–25
Home Rule League 18
house searches 89–90, 91–2
housing 48, 50, 55, 73, 77, 152
Housing Trust 50
human rights 33
Hume, John 143, 158, 163, 164,
     176, 183
hunger strikes 132–5, 138–40

ICI 52
identity 168, 175, 182–3
immigration 15, 17, 30, 152–3
incendiary devices 161
incident centres 124–5
industrial action 119–21, 128
Industrial Revolution 10
industrialization 14–15
insurance claims 159
intelligence operations 122,
     128
internal security strategy
     127–8
internment 32, 95–7, 102, 115
interrogation 32, 97

IRA (Irish Republican Army) 57,
  69, 70, 72, 73–4, 77–9
  British army 89, 99–102, 127–8
  casualties 93, 122
  ceasefire 165
  development of 82–7
  exclusion from formal politics
    116
  hunger strikers 132–5, 138–40
  internment 97
  mainland bombing campaign
    123–4, 144, 158–9, 170
  martial law 92, 94
  murals 134–5, 137
  politics 102–6
  provo psychology 87–90
  SDLP and 115
  splinter groups 184
  supergrass trials 156–7
  truce (1975) 124–30
  violence 94, 98, 106, 125, 128,
    161, see also Sinn Féin
IRB (Irish Republican
  Brotherhood) 81
Ireland Act (1949) 58–9
Irish Labour Party 143
Irish language 178
Irish National League 19
Irish Nationalist Volunteers 24, 82

Jacobite cause 4–6
James II, King 4–6
job discrimination 55–8
Johnson, William 13
judiciary
  abolition of jury trials (1974)
    122

Diplock courts 32, 127
miscarriages of justice 123
supergrass trials 156–7

Keenan, Brian 184
Kingsmill massacre 125, 127

Labour government 132, 172–3,
  176–7, see also individual
  prime ministers
Labour Party
  British 139–40
  Irish 143
  Northern Ireland 40, 49
Lake, General 9
Land League 19
landholdings 1–2
  home rule 18–20
  sectarian competition in
    Armagh 8
  Ulster custom 14
landlords 3, 19, 21
languages 178
Larne 9
Law, Bonar 22
Lemass, Sean 43–4
Lenadoon housing estate, Belfast
  105
Liberal Party 17–25
Libya 157
Liddle, Lieutenant-Colonel D. C.
  57
Lincoln, Abraham 86
linen manufacture 14–15
Lisnaskea 44–5
literature 11–12
Lloyd George, David 25, 34

local government 167
  boundaries 46–7
Londonderry, city of
  Bloody Sunday 97–8
  Bogside siege 71
  civil rights movement 62
  gerrymandering 54–5
  Operation Motorman 106
  partition 28
  sectarian riots 14
  siege in 1689 4–6
  vulnerable Unionist seats in
    44, 45
Londonderry, County 2, 10
Long Kesh prison 97, 105,
  132
Longley, Michael 12
Loyal Orange Institution, *see*
  Orange Order
loyalists 106–12, 178
  bombing campaign 67–8
  casualties 93
  ceasefire 165
  against civil rights movement
    67–9
  internment 97
  murals 136–7
  violence 69–71, 125, 127–8,
    130, 150–1, 160–1, 184
Lynch, Jack 77, 113
Lyons, Tom 47

McCann, Eamonn 87
McCann, Joe 96
McCracken, Henry Joy 9
McCusker, Harold 13
McFarlane, Brendan 'Bic' 139

McGimpsey, Detective Inspector
  Ross 63
McGuinness, Martin 156, 172
McKeague, John 70
McKee, Billy 132
McKenna, Sean 127
McKeown, Ciaran 129
McMonagle, Hugh 88
MacNeice, Louis 11
MacStiofain, Sean 97, 103–4,
  105, 141
Maguire, Frank 138
Maguire, Maria 99, 101
Major, John 167–8, 170
marches
  civil rights 62, 64, 65, 69
  Orange Order 10, 13, 66, 68,
    79, 98–9, 172
  Party Processions Acts 12, 13
  peace 129
  student 69
marriages 1
martial law 92, 94
martial pride 101–2, 108, 130–1
Marxism 78
Mason, Roy 128
Maudling, Reginald 92
Maze, the (*formerly* Long Kesh)
  97, 105, 132
Megaw, R. D. 54
MI6, 125
Middle Liberties Unionist
  Association 50
migration 30, 152–3
Mitchell, George 168, 176
Mitchell Commission 170
Molyneaux, James 142, 150, 151

Monaghan 2
Morrison, Danny 92, 140
Mountbatten, Lord 128
Mowlam, Mo 173
MRF (Military Reconnaissance
    Force) 122
Munro, Henry 9
Munster 9
murals 134–5, 136–7
Murray, Len 119

nationalism
    broad alliance 162–4
    home rule 17–25
    impact of Great War on 26–7
    IRA and 80
    SDLP 114–15, 143
Nazism 85
New Departure alliance 19
New Ireland Forum 143
Newman, Kenneth 127
Newry 14, 65, 69
NICRA (Northern Ireland Civil
    Rights Association) 61
NITAT (Northern Ireland
    Training Team) 122
Nixon, Dr (Unionist MP) 55
no-go areas 96, 106
Nobel Peace Prize 130
Northern Ireland Assembly 116,
    181
Northern Ireland (Emergency
    Provisions) Act (1974) 122
Northern Ireland Labour Party
    (NILP) 40, 59
Northern Ireland Police Service
    181

Nugent, Ciaran 132

oaths of allegiance 59
Obins Street, Portadown 98,
    99
O'Bradaigh, Rurai 141
O'Brien, Conor Cruise 86–7
O'Callaghan, Sean 129
O'Connell, Daniel 9, 10
Officials (IRA wing) 78–9, 125
O'Higgins, Kevin 84
Omagh bomb (1998) 184
Omagh Urban District 47
O'Neill, Terence 29
    attempt to win over some
        Catholics 59–60, 65, 66
    election in 1969, 65
    five-point reform plan 63, 64
    forced from office 70
    Irish unification 43–4
Operation Harvest (1956) 78
Operation Motorman (1972)
    106, 122
opinion polls 158, 159
Orange Order 3
    marches 10, 13, 66, 68, 79,
        98–9, 172
    procession acts 12, 13, see also
        loyalists
OUP (Official Unionist Party)
    118

pacification policies 2–3, 17–20
PAF (Protestant Action Force)
    125
Paisley, Ian 44, 64, 68, 108, 118,
    128, 149, 150

paramilitary organizations, *see*
　　UDA; UVF; IRA
Parliament, Westminster
　　British army involvement 74
　　direct rule 104–5, 113, 121,
　　　131, 132, 141, 148
　　emergency legislation 32–3
　　home rule 18–20
　　Irish members of 9, 10, 13
　　linen manufacture monopoly
　　　14
　　Party Processions Acts 12, 13
　　power-sharing settlement
　　　(1973) 117–21
　　Sinn Féin MPs 28, *see also*
　　　individual governments
Parnell, Charles Stewart 18–20
partition 25, 28–30, 31, 86
Party Processions Acts 12, 13
peace lines, *see* barricades
peace movement 129–30
peace negotiations 53, 175–86
Peacock, Inspector General
　　Joseph Anthony 71–2
peasant movements 8
Peep O Day Boys 8
People's Democracy 60
plantation 2–3
plastic bullets 33, 172
police, *see* RUC (Royal Ulster
　　Constabulary); B-Specials
　　(police auxiliaries)
police reform 178, 186
Portadown 5, 98–9, 172
Post Office 57
power-sharing executive (1973)
　　117–18, 121

Good Friday Agreement
　　(1998) 33, 94, 174, 176–87
Prevention of Terrorism (Temporary
　　Provisions) Act (1974) 33
Prince of Wales regiment 72
prisoners
　　early release of 178, 181, 184
　　hunger strikes 132–5, 138–40
　　internment 32, 95–7, 102, 115
processions, *see* marches
proportional representation 46,
　　116
Protestant Volunteer Force 68–9
Protestants
　　attitude to loyalist violence 111
　　demographic changes 152–3
　　disestablishment of Church of
　　　Ireland 17–18
　　economic advantages 52
　　following partition 31
　　home rule 19–20
　　identity 182–3
　　nationalist republicanism in
　　　1790s 7–9, 10
　　peasant movement 8
　　penal legislation against
　　　Catholics 6
　　plantation policy 3
　　positive discrimination 49–50
　　security forces and 76, 110–11
　　socialist voting fears 38–40
　　in Southern Ireland 49
Provisional IRA, *see* IRA (Irish
　　Republican Army)
psychological torture 96–7
psychological warfare units 122
pub rioting 70

public housing 48, 50, 55
public-order policing 62–3, 68
punishment beatings 175
PUP (Popular Unionist Party)
    112, 171

Queen's University seats 41, 42,
    45

ratepayer's franchise 46–8, 55
Real IRA 184
Redmond, John 21, 25, 80
Rees, Merlyn 119–20, 121, 123,
    125, 127
referenda 168, 180
refugee centres 77
religious liberties 21
rent strikes 19
Republic of Ireland 117, 187
    Anglo-Irish Intergovernmental
        Conference 144–6
    Anglo-Irish Intergovernmental
        Council 131, 142–3
    Anglo-Irish Treaty (1921) 83–4
    anti-partition propaganda 77
    Downing Street Declaration
        (1993) 164
    economic comparisons with
        North 52–3
    Good Friday Agreement
        176–7, 180, 181
    IRA decline in 85
    Protestants in 49
    Sunningdale meeting 117–18,
        146
republicanism 27–8, 80–7, 114,
    see also Sinn Féin

responsibility sharing in local
    government 167
Ribbonmen, Catholic 10
riots 57
    anti-home rule 20
    Belfast 13–14, 16, 17, 72–3,
        76
    civil rights marches sparking
        68
    control methods for 33
    following death of Bobby
        Sands 139
    pub 70
River Bann 49
rolling devolution 131
rope works 15
RUC (Royal Ulster Constabulary)
    32
    casualties 93
    Catholic rioting in Belfast
        (1969) 71, 72–4
    civil rights movement 62–3,
        65, 68
    collusion allegations 125
    lead in anti-terrorist activity
        127, 132
    loyalist marches 172
    rebranding scheme 181
    shoot-to-kill allegations 156–7

Sands, Bobby 133, 138–9
SAS undercover squads 127, 157,
    160
Scotland 2
SDLP (Social Democratic and
    Labour Party) 88, 114–15,
    117, 118, 119, 162, 180

boycott of Anglo-Irish
Intergovernmental Council
131–2
devolution negotiations 176,
178, 187
Forum for Peace and
Reconciliation 171
general election (2001) 185
Northern Ireland Assembly 181
proposal for joint executive
commission 167
Sinn Féin and 140–1, 158
talks with republican
movement 163–4
Second World War 29, 51, 58
security forces 110–11
collusion allegations 125
emergency powers 32, 62
undercover operations 122
settlers 2–3, 8
Shankhill Butchers 110
Shankhill Defence Force 70
Shankhill Road, Belfast 76, 161
shipbuilding industry 15, 51
shoot-to-kill allegations 156
Silent Valley reservoir bombing
69
Sinn Féin 28, 81–2, 102, 116,
121, 124, 162
admitted to peace talks 173
Anglo-Irish Agreement 146
elections for Forum for Peace
and Reconciliation 171
electoral politics 138–41
general election (2001) 185
Good Friday Agreement 178,
180

SDLP and 140–1, 158, 163–4
sidelined in negotiations 176
1641 rebellion 3–4
skilled workers 15
socialism 38–40, 78
Solemn League and Covenant
23–4
Southern Ireland, see Republic of
Ireland
sovereignty 80–1, 84, 115, 141,
143, 144–5
SPA (Special Powers Act) (1922)
32, 62
special category status 132, 134
Spence, Gusty 111
standards of living 52
Stone, Michael 160
Stormont 34–5
economic discrimination
48–55
five-point reform plan 63–4
job discrimination 55–8
Northern Ireland Assembly
116, 181
policy on free demonstration
68
suspension of (1972) 104–5,
113, 149
Unionists seats at 41–2, 44–8
Sunningdale tripartite meeting
(1973) 117–18, 141, 146,
148
supergrass trials 156–7

tarring and feathering 92
Taylor, John 111
television 62, 63, 106, 120

textile mills 15
Thatcher, Margaret 135, 140, 142, 143–4, 144–5, 147, 151
Tone, Wolfe 7
torture 96–7, 110
town planning 53–4, 57
Towns Improvement (Ireland) Act 1854 46
Trimble, David 167, 173, 175, 176, 177, 181, 183, 185, 186
TUAS (Tactical Use of Armed Struggle) 162, 170, 184
Twelfth of July marches 13, 66, 172
twin-track process 168
Tyrie, Andy 119
Tyrone, County 2, 10, 28, 44

UDA (Ulster Defence Association) 99, 107, 109, 119, 160
UDP (Ulster Democratic Party) 112, 171
UDR (Ulster Defence Regiment) 110, 125
UFF (Ulster Freedom Fighters) 107, 161
UKUP (United Kingdom Unionist Party) 171
Ulster-Scots language 178
Ulster Special Constabulary 34
Ulster Volunteer Force, see UVF
unemployment rates 51, 52
unification of Ireland 43–4, 143–4, 146–7, 164, 182
unionism 173, 175
    alienation of grassroots 65–6

Anglo-Irish Agreement 147–53
Boundary Commission 34–5
direct rule preference 141–2, 148
five-point reform plan 63–4
Good Friday Agreement 180
home rule 19–20, 20–5
impact of the Great War 26–7
instability of electoral vote 41–5, 46
joint authority worries 165, 166
Northern Ireland Assembly 183
partition 25, 28–30
power-sharing 117–21
propaganda war to win over Catholics 59–61
ratepayer's franchise 46–8
right wing sectarian provocation 67–8
socialist threat to 38–40, see also DUP; UUP
United Irishmen organization 7, 8, 9, 10
United Nations 146
United States 53, 164–5
Unity Flats, Belfast 70
unskilled workers 15
UUC (Ulster Unionist Council) 21, 117, 118
UUP (Ulster Unionist Party) 141, 142
    DUP and 149, 150
    Forum for Peace and Reconciliation 171

Good Friday Agreement 173,
175, 176, 178, 180, 181, 185
IRA ceasefire 165, 167
power-sharing executive 117,
118
UUUC (United Ulster Unionist
Council) 118–19
UVF (Ulster Volunteer Force)
24, 34, 67, 107, 121, 124
UWC (Ulster Worker's Council)
119, 120–1, 122

Vanguard party 106, 118, 149
vehicle checks 89, 90
veto power 21, 148, 177, 180
Vichy regime 80
victims of violence 72, 76, 93–4,
106, 107, 110, 125, 130, 157
Bloody Sunday 97–8
Enniskillen 159–60
on mainland 123, 159, 170
Omagh bomb 184

Voice of the North (anti-partition
paper) 77
Voster, J. 32

Walker, Reverend George 5–6
Warnock, Edmund 54
water cannons 33
Waterfront Hall 126
weapon decommissioning 167,
168, 170, 171, 173, 181, 184,
185, 186
welfare state 58–9
West, Harry 41, 118, 139
Whitelaw, William 97, 105, 115,
125
William of Orange 4, 136
Williams, Betty 129
Wilson, Harold 63, 113, 120,
127
wool production 14

Young Unionist Movement 151